D1069234

LETTERS FROM THE IRON BRIGADE

GUILD PRESS OF INDIANA, INC.

LETTERS FROM THE IRON BRIGADE

George Washington Partridge, Jr.

1839–1863

Civil War Letters to His Sisters

✳

Hugh L. Whitehouse

Guild Press of Indiana
Indianapolis

First Edition
1994

Guild Press of Indiana, Inc.
6000 Sunset Lane
Indianapolis IN 46208

Library of Congress Number 94-77600

ISBN 1-878208-47-0

ACKNOWLEDGMENTS

STARTING at the beginning, and up to the present, I must acknowledge the recipients of these letters, Celia (Partridge) Slocum and Cordelia (Partridge) Howe, for saving them, out of their affection and remembrance, and for their sense of history, and Justin Partridge Slocum and his sister Rena (Slocum) Lord for their initial genealogical search for and preservation of Partridge records, photographs, bibles, and these very letters, and Helen (Lord) Whitehouse for insisting on saving all of these things, for starting a systematic transcription of the letters, for enthusiastically relating their content, and for enlisting my wife, Martha Whitehouse, to carry on this task, and Martha for finishing transcribing all the letters and distributing the transcriptions to her children and other family members, and for taking up the genealogical trail, and David Slocum Whitehouse for astutely first writing about these letters in their historical context, and Margaret Ferrell for filling in many details on Cordelia Howe's family, and for locating and providing George W. Partridge, Jr.'s 1862 picture, and Alan T. Nolan for his excellent account of the unit in which George W. Partridge, Jr., fought, *The Iron Brigade,* for his reading of the manuscript, and for his general encouragement, and the historian James R. H. Spears for telling me something about Civil War firearms, and for pointing them out to me at the Gettysburg Museum, and Stephen Schuchman, a volunteer in the National Park Service at the Antietam Battlefield, for painstakingly showing me maps and archives there, and Harold L. Miller, Reference Archivist at The State Historical Society of Wisconsin, for extensive catalog information, and Robert C. McKay, researcher in Madison, Wisconsin, for tracking down pertinent information from those catalog listings, and Michael McCormick for his skillful reprographic work, and the staff of The Western Reserve Historical Society Library for my instruction there, and numerous librarians, archivists, and historians, who bear witness to the value of past lives.

❊

George Washington Partridge, Jr.
Seventh Wisconsin Volunteers
Company G
January, 1862

By permission of Agnes Koch

For Martha

CONTENTS

❖

❖

FOREWORD

THE letters here, 27 in all, are a first-hand account of the Civil War experiences of George Washington Partridge, Jr., who enlisted in Wisconsin in August, 1861, fought in a famous brigade in the Army of the Potomac, the Iron Brigade, and died at Gettysburg on July 1, 1863. They are all in his hand, and have been transcribed faithfully, word for word. The framework around them is an attempt to put them in a context in which their meaning can become clearer, so that they can better illuminate his life and times, and increase, in a small way, our knowledge of the war. This framework is pieced together from a number of sources.

The first of these sources is a verbal account, passed down through four generations. He was my great-grandmother's brother, my mother's mother's mother's brother. This is a slight and somewhat sketchy source, one I heard since childhood from my mother and my grandmother, but one of lore and myth which has made him familiar and real; they often referred to him in the first person as a family member, as, simply, George.

A second source is a family search started by my grandmother and her brother early this century, and carried forward exhaustively in scholarly genealogical detail by my wife, Martha Whitehouse. What interested Martha in searching in my family were specifically the obvious strong bonds, absent in her own family, of those westward-moving pioneers who had little else to hang onto except their relatives, bonds which seemed to carry down to my generation, who had a great-great-uncle named George who long ago fought bravely and died young.

A third source is composed of relevant historical records and accounts of the war. A number of these are cited in the footnotes. Foremost and essential among these is an excellent book on the history of the brigade in which George Partridge served, *The Iron Brigade,* by Alan T. Nolan, published by Macmillan in 1961, a second edition by The State Historical Society of Wisconsin in 1975, and a third edition by the Historical Society of Michigan in 1983. I have referred often to Mr. Nolan's book throughout.

A fourth source comes from visiting the sites where Partridge camped and fought, and from walking on that ground where he walked, where this is possible. The fields at Gainesville (Brawner Farm), South Mountain, Antietam, and Gettysburg afford some imaginative scope, some feel, some view of his experience there, but in most places this sort of direct view is obscured by newer buildings, roads, traffic, and commerce, and simply by the rush of natural change from the growth of trees and brush, from erosion, and from the silt of time. The collected artifacts of battle at these places also provide insight, as do the resident experts, and visiting experts as well. On a gray June day in 1936, at a nearly deserted Gettysburg battlefield, I stood with my grandmother, my first expert, in the rain on Little Round Top, where she swept her arms about and pointed out with conviction what had really happened there.

A fifth source for the framework surrounding the letters comes from analysis of the content of the letters themselves, for interpretation of Partridge's motives, his state of mind, his character, and its growth over the 17 months from first letter to last. Some of this interpretation is speculative, of course, and other readers may have different insights.

Partridge wrote from the army to his sisters in Erie, Pennsylvania, and in Waukegan, Illinois. The Erie letters were to Celia Slocum,[1] my great-grandmother, 12 years older than Partridge, and to Evaline Slocum,[2] 14 years older than Partridge, and married to Celia Slocum's father-in-law. This group of Erie letters was passed down directly from mother to daughter. The Waukegan letters were to Cordelia Howe,[3] two years older than Partridge, and to Phebe Holdridge,[4] 11 years older than Partridge. These Waukegan letters were passed down by Cordelia Howe to my grandmother's brother,

---

[1] Celia Maria (Partridge) Slocum, 1827-1902.

[2] Betsey Evaline (Partridge) Slocum, 1825-?

[3] Cordelia Sophia (Partridge) Howe, 1837-1920, known as Dele, which Partridge sometimes spelled Deal.

[4] Eunice Phebe Williams (Partridge) Holdridge, 1828-?

who, as I mentioned, was searching for his roots, and from thence to my grandmother, to my mother, to my wife. The letters are in a clear hand, most of them in ink. Partridge obviously had elementary schooling, and his father was literate, and probably his mother. Partridge wrote regularly to his parents in Wisconsin, and probably to a fifth sister, Jane Partridge.[5] He also wrote to two cousins. The whereabouts of these letters to his parents, to Jane Partridge, and to his cousins, is unknown to us.

A note on Partridge's family. George Washington Partridge, Sr., was born in Preston, Connecticut, in 1802, and was named, as were many children of the time, in honor of the most famous American, who had died in 1799. (To further illustrate the topical naming practices of the day, George Partridge, Sr.'s, uncle, born in 1776, was also named George Washington Partridge. His aunt Peace Partridge was born in 1778.) In the westward movement of New Englanders following the Revolution and the War of 1812, the Partridge family and a number of their relatives left their ancestral homes in Connecticut and struck out across New York State, stopping for several years in Hartwick, New York, near Cooperstown, where George Partridge, Sr., met Betsey Morris of Fly Creek. They were married in 1824, and Evaline and Celia were born there. The family proceeded farther west, stopping briefly in Allegany County, New York, where Phebe was born, and then on to Wesleyville, just east of Erie, Pennsylvania, by the early 1830's, where Catharine, Jane, and Cordelia were born before George Jr. was born in 1839. One more daughter, Mary Ellen, was born in 1841. Catharine and Mary Ellen had died before Partridge went to war.

George Partridge, Sr., was a carpenter. It is likely his father was also a carpenter, although there is no direct record, since many local Connecticut records of the late eighteenth century were burned. But four of George Partridge, Sr.'s, six brothers and a brother-in-law were carpenters, indicating a family occupation. In the early 1850's, the Partridges again moved to the west, to Waukegan, Illinois. Celia and Evaline married in Erie and stayed there. Seeking work, or land,

[5] Sarah Ann Jane Partridge, 1835-1894.

or opportunity, the family moved again, in 1856, to Mosinee, Wisconsin, a few miles below Wausau. Cordelia and Phebe married and stayed in Waukegan. George Partridge, Sr., bought two lots in Mosinee, and built a house for his family. They were not well off, and at the outbreak of the war George Partridge, Jr., was living and working away from home with a laborer,[6] perhaps a lumberman, who had married Partridge's younger sister, Mary Ellen, in 1860.

Abraham Lincoln was elected President on November 6, 1860. The South Carolina legislature, fearing the abolition of slavery under the Republicans, unanimously passed an Ordinance of Secession on December 20, 1860, dissolving the union between the State of South Carolina and the other States.[7] In February, 1861, six other states joined with South Carolina. Lincoln took office on March 4, and urged reconciliation. On April 12, Confederate artillery opened fire on Fort Sumter, an island fort off Charleston, South Carolina. On April 15, Lincoln called for a volunteer 90-day militia of 75,000 men to resist the rebellion and to preserve the Union. The response was overwhelming. Wisconsin, asked to supply an infantry regiment, had assembled two by the first week in May. Also in May, volunteers were asked to change their three-month enlistments to three years, and most went along.

Partridge signed up for three years on August 15, 1861, at Grand Rapids,[8] Wisconsin, and his Wood County company became Company G of the Seventh Regiment, Wisconsin Volunteers, one of ten companies making up the Regiment, each company composed of a captain, two lieutenants, 13 noncommissioned officers, two musicians, a wagoner, and eighty-plus privates.[9] The Seventh trained

---

[6] Joseph Tanguey

[7] Henry Steele Commager, *The Blue and the Gray* (New York: Bobbs-Merrill, 1950), pp. 5-7. The Ordinance, printed therein, declares emphatically and at length that the anticipation of the abolition of slavery is the reason for secession.

[8] Now Wisconsin Rapids.

[9] Mark M. Boatner III, *The Civil War Dictionary* (New York: David McKay Company, 1959), entry ORGANIZATION, p. 612.

briefly at Camp Randall in Madison, Wisconsin, and on September 21st left for Washington by train, 1,106 men strong, including a regimental staff of fifteen, headed by a colonel, lieutenant colonel, and major.[10]

There are virtually no reasons given in Partridge's letters for his joining the army. Slavery or its abolition is never an issue. Partridge is not naïve. He reads newspapers, and certainly knew about North-South issues. Slavery is simply outside of his experience. Wisconsin had just become a State in 1848, however, and there was strong Union feeling there. A great number of young Wisconsin men had already answered Lincoln's call. Six regiments, some 6,000 men, and most of a seventh, had already joined from Wisconsin. Wisconsin records state that he was enlisted into service by Captain S. Stevens. He may have been actively recruited, a common practice of the day. He was, however, a volunteer, and proud of the fact. He listed his regiment as the *7th Reg^t W. V.*, short for *Wisconsin Volunteers*. His first four letters here carry elaborate letterheads, some in color, stating THE CONSTITUTION AND THE UNION, UNION, and OUR COUNTRY'S DEFENDERS. The chances are he was caught up in the spirit of the time, and thought that going to fight for his country would be an adventure, and worthwhile.

My mother first transcribed the Erie letters, unconsciously correcting some of the spelling and punctuation. Martha Whitehouse typed these, and transcribed and typed the Waukegan letters years later when they reached her from my mother. I have gone over all of these, comparing them to the original letters. Partridge was very chary of all punctuation marks and seemed to have his own code for capitalizing. He very rarely used commas, and only occasionally used periods. Directions for longer temporal pauses, or shifts in thought, or special emphasis, were indicated sometimes by a double period.. To save paper, he sometimes indicated paragraphs by leaving a line unfilled and starting the next line without indenting. I have preserved all of the original spelling in the letters, all of the capitals, and all of the marks. Following Martha's practice, I have put spaces at

---

[10] *Ibid.*

the end of all sentences, including those which end in periods or double periods. Some ambiguity remains when a sentence ends at the end of a transcribed line, but such ambiguity is in the original, too. In a few places I have supplied a word in brackets where Partridge left one out by accident. Purists may ignore these. Where a line is not filled, and could have been, I have ended a paragraph and started a new one. I have indented the paragraphs a standard amount, but have tried to preserve the original spacing at the heading and especially at the close, where format seems to imply expression.

IN CAMP NEAR WASHINGTON

1.   Phebe Holdridge and Cordelia Howe   (Waukegan)

Arlington hights
O 13 1861

*Dear sister   Doubtless you have heard I was in the army before
this time   well I am here   I enlisted in a company at Grand
Rapids some time in August   Stayed there about two weeks and
went to Madison   Stayed on camp ground there about a month
and drilled   I did not go into the city while I stayd there.. well
we started from there about ten oclock on Saturday   I have forgot
what day of the month it was but we came by way of Janesville to
Chicago   arrived in Chicago about eight P.M.*

*we was to have a supper there but it was not got for us   but as
it hapened we had something of our own to eat   we marched two
miles through the city and it was warm and dusty.   well we got to
the cars and waited for them to start and they did not start until
twelve oclock   from Chicago we came by way of fort wayne to
Pitsburg   there we got a good warm breakfast   at fort wayne we
got some warm coffee   we road first class cars to Harisburg and
from there through to Washington we rode in freight cars   from
Pitsburg to Harisburg was the rufest country I ever saw   the
railroad follows a river   I dont know how far but we road more
than half a day in the valley   just before dark we went thrugh a
tunnel under the ground I should think about a mile long*

*as I said before we road in freight cars Harisburg to Washing-
ton   we arrived at Baltimore about seaven pm and marched
thrugh the city about two miles and half and stayed all night in the
depot   in the morning we started on for the big city   we arrived
there little after noon   went to a place they called soldiers retreat
and got something to eat   I think the place was rightly named for
the soldiers would retreat from all such places   all we got to eat
there was a small peace of bread and some stinken pork but you
may guess we did not eat much of it.   well night came and we
were ordered to stay all night there so we unrolled our blankets*

and laid down to sleep about ten oclock the order came from the major to sling knapsacks. most of them was asleep but such another scrambling you never heard of before one was looking for a gun another was looking for something else some said we had got to march nine miles that night out to the 5th regiment that there was was there and we had got to be there by daylight the next morning well we marched about a mile and halted before a large building then marched in and took off our knapsacks and laid down for the night there was a fire in the city that night but we could not get out it burned two small buildings..

the next day we marched about two hours in the city to show ourselfs and then marched a mile out of town on the camp ground and waited for our tents before we got them piched it began to rain and we had to pich them in the rain

There was another Regt there that was going to move the next day so we piched our tents the quickest way we could until they moved then we piched on their ground.. after we had been there a week we moved out to chain bridge and camped by the [camp] of the 6th Regt after we had been there a few days we were ordered to march for Arlington Hights where we are now.. last night we had another husle there was a dispatch sent in for us to be ready to march any time at ten munites notice and they thought we had got to march in ten munites and they all got ready in a little less than no time we may start from here tonight and we may not start for a week.. there was a balloon started up a few miles from here this morning and came over here before it got over here it went above the clouds and was out of sight nearly five munites when it came in sight it was a good way off it went very fast well I dont think of much more to write at present so good buy direct your letter to Company G 7th Regt W. V. Arlington Hights care of Capt Stevens you must write soon as you get this you must let Cordelia read it and tell her I will write to her next time good night yours affectionately

    E P Holdridge   Geo W Partridge jr

This is quite voluble for Partridge. He knew he had started on a great adventure. Partridge writes very simply and colloquially, with no literary flourishes. At 22, he is mature, good-natured, open, not prone to exaggerate nor embellish. True to his New England fore-bears, he tends to stay in control, understating his emotions, letting his reader draw her own response from what he has selected to report. He is sorting out his new experiences by explaining them to his familiar community, his family. He is not writing for posterity, but for these two sisters alone. He assumes their affection and good will, and in his easy way, sustains it, and sustains himself, as he would by visiting friends. Today, he would use the telephone.

The Seventh Wisconsin was assigned to General Rufus King's Brigade, consisting of four regiments. In addition to the Seventh Wisconsin, there were the Second and Sixth Wisconsin, and the Nineteenth Indiana. Though not an all-Wisconsin brigade, it was a Western brigade in an Eastern army, the Army of the Potomac, under the command of 34 year-old General George B. McClellan. The Army of the Potomac was organized into divisions at this time, and General King's Brigade was one of three under General Irvin McDowell.

The Seventh Wisconsin Regiment was the last of the four to join King's Brigade, and only one, the Second Wisconsin, had been in battle. In July, 1861, in the Brigade of General William T. Sherman, the Second Wisconsin fought well but fled in the general confusion in the First Battle of Bull Run, losing 23 dead, 65 wounded, and 63 captured.

The Arlington Heights, Virginia, camp was Fort Tillinghast, near the home of Robert E. Lee. The army was to stay there until March.

The balloon Partridge reports seeing is probably a military bal-loon. Hydrogen balloons were used for observation in McClellan's Peninsular Campaign in the spring of 1862.[11]

---

[11] Geoffrey C. Ward, *The Civil War: an illustrated history* (New York: Alfred A. Knopf, 1990), pp. 112, 130.

2.   Celia Slocum and Evaline Slocum   (Erie)

Camp Arlington
Dec 15 1861

*Dear sisters Evaline & Celia   I presume you have heard before
this time that I was in the survice of the U. S.   I am here   I have
been here for some time   I did not write to you but I dont know
why unless it was because I did not want to   I am not much of a
hand to write and I have not much of a table or stand to write on
I have my bed for a chair and my knee for a table so you can guess
what kind of a chance I have for writing   well this is not giving
much of the news   I dont know as there is much to write about
we have not [had] any battle with the rebels yet but we had one
with our selves   a regular performance of a battle   I wish we
had had balls in our guns and the rebels standing before us and
then see them fall but they were not there   may be we will have a
chance after a while   at lest I hope so..   We had a grand review a
short time ago where there was from 75 to 80 thousand men on
the field   it was the grandest sight I ever saw and I guess you
would say so if you had been there..   We were out to the front on
picket guard a few days ago but did not see any rebels   one man
said he seen two men cros his path one night   he chalenged them
twice who goes there and fired his gun at them but did not kill any
one and I guess he did not see any one   the 6th Regt was out
there before we was and they seen a barn advancing on them
they all fired on it and retreated back into the woods   I dont
know wether the barn followed them or not   that is what our
Colonel told us and I dont dispute his word..   there was a man
dyed in our company a few days ago with the quick consumption
I will tell you a little how the funerals go on here   the band goes
the ambulance next with the corps and three men on each side of it
behind that is eight men with guns followed by the remander of
the company   the drums have a black silk handkercheif over the
head and the snairs tied so that they wont sound   when the grave*

*was filled we fired the guns three times over the grave   well has
the poet said solemmly rolled the muffled drums   well there is not
much sound of war here   at present every thing is still.*

*   well I dont think of any more to write this time..   I suppose
you have heard that Father got hurt   it was a bad fall and I have
done all I can to help him at present   well my paper is groing
short and I shall have to stop or it will not have enough to finish
in   good night from your only affectionate brother*
Geo W Partridge
to his sisters C. M. S. & E. S.

Partridge is a little more formal in writing to these two older
sisters in Erie. Celia Slocum is 34, the mother of five (two others had
died in their first year), and Evaline Slocum is 36; Partridge had left
Erie some ten years before. He apologizes for not writing earlier, but
it seems he has not written to them very often or at all ("I am not
much of a hand to write"), but plainly wants to make contact.

He is eager to fight. He wants action. This will not always be the
case. He makes light of picket duty, and jokes about apprehensive
soldiers who shoot at shadows. Partridge's humor often sounds like
social banter, and this probably was. He is good at relating it, which
indicates to me his social ease among peers. He implies that seeing
shadows is part of learning what is truly to be feared. He is learning
courage himself, and bonding with his comrades as well. In contrast,
another private soldier of the Seventh Wisconsin writes home about
picket duty, "It did not happen to fall my lot to go but I volunteered
my services for there were some that did not want to run the risk of
getting a hole punched through them.... I tell you it is rather lone-
some to march out from ones company about 6 or 8 rods in the dead
of night towards the enemy. It is rather risky business. There has
been some soldiers shot most evey night but we came in safe and
sound."[12]

---

[12] Horace Currier, Pvt., Company I, Seventh Regiment, Wisconsin Volunteers, Currier MSS, State Historical Society of Wisconsin, p. 1, letter to his
brother Edwin, December 16, 1861.

Partridge's father broke his thigh bone and his wrist in a fall. His thigh bone (or hip) never healed properly, ending his career as a carpenter. The army pay Partridge sent home became his parents' sole income. After the war, his father applied for a Federal pension for the loss of support from his son, and received one. After his father's death, his mother also applied for and received a Federal pension.

The following letter to Cordelia Howe and Phebe Holdridge in Waukegan is written on stationery probably purchased in Washington. It has an engraving of the United States Capitol across the top showing the finished new dome, in construction during the war. Below the engraving are blanks to fill in, identifying the sender's unit.

3.   Cordelia Howe and Phebe Holdridge   (Waukegan)

Head **Headquarters** *7th* **Regt.,***W.V.* **Camp** *Arlington* **Co.** *G*
                                    December 21 **1861**

*Dear Sisters   I recieved your letter some time ago but as there
was not much news to write I did not answer rite off and there is
not much more news now.   there was a man taken out of this
Regiment yesterday for committing a murder in iowa before he
joined the army   I did not hear the particulars only that he was
taken out and put in irons   I dont think he was very smart for
they said he wrote home to his wife in iowa and sent his likeness
to her and they found where he was by that.*

*   this Regt was out on picket guard out to the front lines since I
wrote before   no rebels to be seen   one man thought he saw two
men one night and took them to be rebels because they did not
stop when [he] told them to   he fired his gun at them but did not
kill nor hurt any one (and I guess he did not see any one)   the
6th Regt. was out there before we was and they did not see any rebels   our Colonel said the sixth saw a barn advanceing on them
and they all fired on it and retreated back into the woods   I dont
know wether the barn followed them or not   the Colonel did not
say but wanted to know if we seen any such thing coming after us
(No)   we have had three suit of cloths since we came in the army
one cotten suit & one grey wool suit in camp Randel and one
blew suit since we came here   the boys [are] going to send a part
of their grey suit home and I think I will send mine home to as we
have no use for them here and we are not allowed to ware them
on drill   I have a grey overcoat grey jacket and the cotten jacket
that I shal not use and if I ever get home they will do me some
good   and if I dont they will do some one else some good and if I
keep them here we may be ordered to march and have to leave
them and maybe never see them again   they say though that we
can box them up and send them over to the City and have [them]*

taken [care] of for us but I dont like the plan for we may never see them again..

I bought a paper tonight which had some good news in it there was news of a skirmish a little ways from here   you will [see]the news of it in the paper if you take any   I want to send the paper home   the fight was not more that ten or twelve miles from here..

well we have not had any battle with the rebels yet and I dont know as we [will] have but I hope we may advance before a great while..   well I will have to get another sheet for this is groing short

I thought I could write all I wanted to in a half sheet but there is one thing more   you spoke of sending your babys likeness and wanted to know which one I wanted   I guess I will take delly this time that is if you send it and wait till your other girl gets biger..   I dont know which one I directed my last letter to but I will direct this to you

      C. S. Howe
and you must let P read it   from your brother
      Geo W Partridge
to his sisters C. S. H. and E. P. H.
excuse all bad writing and mistake

Well here is another peace..   we have plenty of blankets to sleep under   have two apeace   that is[,] all that wanted them and there is two of [us] sleeps together so that we have four blankets over [us] if we want   we generally get cedar brush to lay on if we can get them handy and if not get some other kind   I thought when I got down here I would be out of the pinery but not so   for when we was out on picket we were in as thick pine woods as I ever saw   it was not large trees but they stood close together

Well I have not excused myself for not sending my likeness and I dont know if there is any excuse   but I will tell you I had not money to spare after sending home what I did   I was over in the city and in the Capitol   it is the finest peace of workmanship I

*ever saw or ever will see I guess   I had not time to go all over it
and did not see much else   but nevermind   I will get some more
money before a great while and then see   I sent my money home
on account of father being hurt   well I shal have to close before
long   tell Howe I send him my best respects and when he gets in
the army again to write me and tell me where to direct and I will
write to him   I dont feel like writing much more tonight so I
guess I will close   good night*

from your brother
Geo W Partridge

The advancing barn obviously appealed to Partridge, but a good
story bears repeating. The concern for saving the extra uniforms
reflects the scarcity of property in Partridge's frontier upbringing.
Also, private's pay is $13 a month, and Partridge is sending most of
that home. Partridge has a mature sense of his own mortality: "...if I
ever get home they will do me some good   and if I dont they will
do some one else some good...." He is not sentimental, and at this
time expresses no fear of the risk of battle.

Cordelia Howe's daughter Edith Adell (delly) is nearly three; the
new baby, Cora Ella, is a month old. Cordelia Howe's husband,
William Howe,[13] is 40, a carpenter by trade. He is a musician in the
Western army. Phebe Holdridge's husband, Ira Holdridge, a farmer,
is 64, nearly twice Phebe's age.

---

[13] William Harrison Howe, 1820-1901.

4.   Celia Slocum   (Erie)

Camp Arlington
Jan 11   1862

Dear sister C.
I receaved your letter dated 29 and was much rejoyced to hear
from you and hear of your good health   I am well at present and
have been ever since I joined the army..   I dont see as there is any
more sign of battle now than there was when I enlisted nor as
much   the army here is all lying still and has been ever since we
have been on this ground which is about five months..   this Regt
has been on picket twice   I presume you have never been on
picket but have been through picket but there was not as much
danger there as here where no one can go through without a cer-
tain signal   you speak of Richards going into the fishing business
I wish I was there to help him   not that I am sick of the army   I
think I am doing as much good here as any where or will be in
course of time but I always liked fishing business and hope he may
do well.

Christmas and New years was spent here about as dull as I
ever saw it spent   there was nothing going Christmas and not
much more New years   the sutler treated us to the oysters New
years and that was about all
you speak of the Erie Regt   there is quite a number of the
Penn Regts around here but I dont know where they were got up
there is one about two miles and a half from here   that is the 83
Regt I believe   I herd that was Camped in Erie and the Colo-
nel[14] *had been a lawyer there for a good while   I dont know*

---

[14] The Colonel was Col. James W. McLane, killed at Gaine's Mill in the Peninsular Campaign, June 27, 1862. The Eighty-third Pennsylvania had an illustrious history. At Gettysburg, it was part of the Third Brigade, First Division, Fifth Corps, a brigade led by Col. Strong Vincent, also from Erie, who secured Little Round Top on July 2, 1863, where he was mortally wounded. He was a hero at Gettysburg, and became a hero in Erie, where a high school was named for him. My grandmother, born in Erie in 1869, Celia Slocum's youngest

how it is I have not been over there yet   if you will tell me what Regt I will try and find it if it is here

I have not said much about the wether yet   we had about an inch of snow last sunday and it lasted two days when it began to rain and rained most of the time for two days and now the mud is shoe deep any where out doors.   it is warm and pleasant today.. as for sending you papers I cant do it now as I have not a cent of money to buy them with   but pay day is close at hand   I think we will be payd off next week some time and then I will send some..   I sent the most of my money home before and did not have enough for my own use   I think I will not send quite as much this time.   well I dont think of much more to write this time.   tell Evaline she must write as often as she can.   give my best respects to Ben and wife and all the rest of the folks

from your only Brother in the army

Geo. W. Partridge

to his sister Celia. M. Slocum

Richard Slocum, 36, is Celia's husband. At this time the Slocums are living in Manchester, nine miles west of Erie, on Walnut Creek, less than a mile from Lake Erie. Slocum has tried a number of occupations, none of them very successful. Commercial fishing on Lake Erie is a viable enterprise, but not for Slocum. Partridge's wish to be of help sounds genuine; he may guess from his Erie days that Slocum will not succeed on his own. His speculation that he is doing as much good in the army as he would anywhere, or will be, is as strong an expression of his motivation for being in the army as he will make, and typical of his reluctance to talk about his feelings.

---

child, heard and read about him in school; it was no doubt *his* deeds and those of his brigade she was pointing out in the rain on Little Round Top in June, 1936, although I was unaware of it then.

5.   Phebe Holdridge and Cordelia Howe   (Waukegan)

Headquarters *Seaventh*   **Regt.***Wis. Vol.*   **Camp** *Arlington.*
Co. G.
Jan 27 1862

Dear sisters
*   It has been some time since I receaved your last letter dated 7 but I will try and make some excuse for not writing sooner   in the first place there was no news to write about and I wanted to wait until I got my likeness to send.. it has been very muddy here for the last week and is not over with yet   we called it muddy when I lived in Waukegan but I think now there is no mud there the roads are so bad that the teams cant travel here   there was two horses killed here a few days ago.   one of them broke two of his legs and they killed him the other was killed by running away by some way he fell down and stuck a stick in his brest and killed him.   I guess the roads are rather worse here than other places for it is level and no chance for the water to run off.*
*   Some of the prisoners that were taken at the Bull Run fight have returned   there is quite a number in the 2 Wis   they say they were treated rather cruel in Richmond   were not allowed to put their heads out of the prison windows nor hardly to look out.. one of the prisoners said there was two men shot dead for looking out the window..   he said they had a roll call of the prisoners twise ever day and if a man did not answer to his name the first time they would draw a pistol and threaten to shoot him if he ever done it again..*
*   you must not think it is strange because I do not write more about the army affairs for there is nothing worth speaking of here some of the boys seem to think the army will move as quick as it freeses up or drys up but I dont see any sign of it yet..   well they are calling for dinner*
*   P. M.   there has been quite a number of men died in this Regt since we came on this ground.   there have been three out of this*

Company   the last was a young man by the name of Jones   he was sick in the hospital three weeks   had no relation in the company that I know of

well I dont think of much more to write this time   we have had no snow here of any account yet   it frose a little last night but is thawing out fast today   but it dont help the mud any   well I guess I will close by saying I send you my likeness this time   I will send Deals in another envelop.. excuse all mistakes and bad writing for the wind blows very hard and shakes the tent so that I could hardly write what I have

[fro]m your only Brother in the army
[Geo. W.]Partridge
[E. P.]Holdridge

With 75-80,000 soldiers with horses, wagons, and artillery, and with all the necessary support services and equipment camped in a large field, it is no wonder that the rain and snow of winter bring mud. This whole region becomes virtually impassable for the armies each winter. Partridge's comparison of Washington's mud with Waukegan's is expressive, spoken deadpan, but eliciting a smile, another example of Partridge's colloquial facility. He was probably well-liked in camp. The exchange or parole of prisoners is fairly common early in the war. Partridge is skeptical of the army's moving soon, and he will prove correct.

Sickness took a heavy toll on the brigade. Nolan writes that "In February, 263 of the 3,669 men in the brigade reported sick. Although measles and other trivial complaints were often at fault, fatalities were not uncommon, as evidenced by the death of almost sixty of the Hoosiers and an additional seventeen men of the Seventh Wisconsin. The death rate was exceeded only by the rate of discharge for illness. In the Sixth Wisconsin alone, eighty-five enlisted men were mustered out during the winter."[15] Partridge complains in one letter of a sore back, but apparently was never sick.

The letter is torn at the bottom through the closing.

---

[15] Alan T. Nolan, *The Iron Brigade* (New York: Macmillan, 1961), p. 35.

6.   Cordelia Howe   (Waukegan)

Camp Arlington
Jan 28 1862

Dear sister   I send you my likeness in this small letter as you will
see if you get it   I wrote to P and sent one to her and you can
read the news   I hope you will not wait so long before you
[write] as I did   for if you do I shall think you did not get this
and write again   tell P so   for I guess I did not put it in her let-
ter   write as soon as you can and send your likeness
                    from your only Brother
                    Geo. W. Partridge

                to his sister C. S. Howe

The fold lines of this letter indicate a picture two-and-three-quarters inches wide, probably a tintype in a paper mask. Partridge indicates in his next letter (letter 7) that he had four taken. He has sent one each to Phebe Holdridge and Cordelia Howe. He probably sent one to his parents in Mosinee. I have heard most of my life of a picture of George W. Partridge, Jr., which my grandmother had, presumably from her mother, Celia Slocum, which was lent to another relative in the 1930's and disappeared. A search has gone on for this picture for years, and continues, but it has not been found.

In 1991, in the course of genealogical research, Martha Whitehouse received from a descendant[16] of Cordelia Howe a photographic copy of a tintype purported to be of George W. Partridge, Jr. That picture appears here in the Frontispiece.

---

[16] Margaret Ferrell, of Crofton, Kentucky. She is a descendant of Cordelia Howe's first child, Edith Adell Howe, 1859-1931, "delly" of letter 3.

7.   Phebe Holdridge   (Waukegan)

Camp Arlington
Feb 19 1862

Dear Sister
  having nothing els to do I take this opportunity to answer your letter of the 15th which I have just received this eav   the likenesses came through all safe and I was very glad to get them   you spoke of mine looking so Cross.   I dont know what made me look so cross   I am shure I tryed to look good natured   I had four taken and they all looked just exactly alike   but that is enough of that   turn over and say something els
  well I will try and answer some of your questions.
  as for the papers I guess I have plenty of these but I would like one from there now and then   there is six or dosen more or less newspaper pedlars here every morning   I sent one to deal a few days ago and will send more..
  well as for the leasure time   I read some of the time   sleep some.   we have a small fire place in the tent   have to carry wood from half to three quarters of a mile or go without and that takes some time   and the remander of the time I eat..   we have bread salt pork salt beef fresh beef rice homeny beans coffee sugar molasses tea and candles
  there is some sick here   I do not know exactly how many   there is two from this Company in the hospital   there is a great many in the city hospitals   I will send you a paper with the lists when it comes..
  well as for the mud   I dont [know] as there can be any more than there was when I wrote before but it has been raining ever since.   well I wont make it any wors than it is but it has rained some and snowed a little and it is raining now   but I dont think the mud can get any wors..
  well I believe that is all the questions you asked and I dont think of any more to answer.

*well I suppose you get all the war news before I could send it.
there is not much going on here   no sign of a movement of this
army.. well there is no more news to write this time..*

*you did not say wether deal got my likeness or not   I hope she
did   and you did not say wether she was going to write or not
therefore I direct this to you.   I beleave that is all this time
write as often as you can   not wait as long as they do at Erie
good night*

from your Brother
Geo. W. Partridge
E. P. Holdridge

Although the picture in the Frontispiece is labelled George
Washington Partridge, Jr., it carries no identifying label from its
time. There is solid genealogical evidence it came down from Cordelia and William Howe. Howe had two sons from a previous mar-
riage, but they would be 11 and 13 in 1862. Surprisingly, both did
serve in the West as extremely young soldiers; the younger son,
Lysten Drewitt Howe, enlisted as a musician when he was 10, and
was reputed by some to be the drummer boy of Shiloh.[17] But this
picture is hardly that of an 11 year-old or of an adolescent. Partridge
would be 22 in January of 1862, and this is quite consistent with the
picture. He has on a dark blue frock coat common in the Army of
the Potomac, which he mentions in letter 3. (A telling feature of the
soldiers of the Iron Brigade is a tall black hat with a large black
feather or plume, called the Hardee hat, worn by many officers. The
black hats make soldiers of the Brigade look larger than life, particu-
larly to Confederate eyes, but it is not until May, when John Gibbon
takes command of the brigade, that these special hats are issued.)
Partridge is described in the Company enlistment records as 21

---

[17] Lysten D. Howe enlisted with his father in the Fifteenth Illinois, in 1861.
He got the measles, was discharged, and reenlisted in February, 1862, in the
Fifty-fifth Illinois. His father arranged to transfer to the Fifty-fifth, and served
there with his two sons. Others claimed to be the drummer boy of Shiloh; Lysten
D. Howe did not, though he served at Shiloh, and presumably played his drum
there. This information also came from Margaret Ferrell.

years of age, single, blue eyes, brown hair, fair complexion, 5 feet 5 inches in height, occupation, a lumberman. Facial features in the picture resemble those of his sisters, of whom there are a number of extant photographs. But the final and convincing evidence of the genuineness of this picture is Phebe Holdridge's assertion that he looks so Cross. A more severe-looking 22 year-old never sent his picture home. Not just one. He "had four taken [there were no duplicate prints from single negatives—the tintype itself was the negative, and was reversed, as is the "US" on his belt buckle] and they all looked just exactly alike." He does not want to talk further directly about himself. "...that is enough of that."

There is no question that Partridge is bored. In his free time he reads the paper, carries wood, and eats. Sickness continues. Mud continues. He sees no sign of movement.

8.   Cordelia Howe   (Waukegan)

Camp Arlington
Mar 9 1862

*Dear sister   I take this opportunity to answer your last letter
dated 4 which I receaved two days ago..   we are all well in the
Company except th[r]ee or four and they are not bad enough to
go to the hospital..   well I dont know as there is much news to
write except it is a fine warm day   the warmest we have had
since last fall   but expect a rain storm day after tomorro when I
come on Guard.*

*most of the boys think that we will move in a few days.   well
I dont know but we will.   there is some performances going on
here that looks like it.   one thing in particular.   all the men that
are not able to stand a march have to go over to the city Hospital
and they have gave us some small tents to carry with us   the tents
are about six feet square and two men to a tent   they are made so
each man carrys half of the tent   they are made just to keep the
rain off at night..*

*we have receaved some new rifles since I wrote before   they
are called the austrian Rifles.   and I think they are a good gun.
we went out and tryed them a few days ago   we shot 40 rods at a
ring one foot across and a good many hit the mark   I think it was
good shooting..*

*well a little in answer to your letter   about your likeness   if
you have got it taken I think you better send it   it will suit me
just as well at present..   and about the money for Jane   I can pay
her next pay day which will be in a few days..   well I cant think
of much more to write only I wish this War was over   I am not
home sick but am tired of staying in close quarters..   if the army
of the Potomac ever advances I have an oppinion there will be a
considerable fight   but all I have got to say is the sooner it Comes
the quicker it will be over.   and I am ready for it..*

well I dont think of any more this time.. yes one word more
I mailed a paper to you this morning..
   I can just as well write a letter to each of you   I have plenty of
time to answer all the letters I get and more if I could get them..
      well good night for this time
      from your Brother
         Geo.W.Partridge

   to his Sister   C. S. Howe

At last it seems that the army will move. The new rifles issued to
the Seventh Wisconsin are Austrian "Lorenz" model 1854 rifle-
muskets. General Irvin McDowell, in command of the division,
reported to Army Headquarters in January that the Seventh Wisconsin muskets were Springfield Altered Smooth. He also stated
that "The muskets of the Seventh Wisconsin are reported as bad, and
that the men lack confidence in them."[18] Rifled gun barrels have
long, spiral grooves inside which impart spin to the bullet, giving it
gyroscopic stability so that it flies straight, analogous to a hard,
tightly-spiralled football pass. A smooth barrel, without rifling,
imparts no spin, so that the unstabilized bullet may fly randomly off
course, somewhat like a knuckleball pitch in baseball. The new Austrian rifles were far more accurate than the smoothbores they replaced. The Springfield Smoothbores were 1816 models, manufac-
tured until 1840. U.S. arsenals had many in stock at the start of the
war, and many were issued. They were nearly 57 inches long and
weighed nine pounds. They had been altered from a flintlock to a
percussion cap ignition system, which did not improve their accuracy, but cut down on misfires. 40 rods is 220 yards, one-eighth of a
mile. One would be unlikely to hit a one-foot diameter target at that
distance with a smoothbore musket. Smoothbores rarely even had

---

[18] *War of Rebellion, Official Records of the Union and Confederate Armies*
(Washington: Government Printing Office, 1882-1900), 5, 708.

rear sights. Considering that 90% of Civil War battlefield casualties came from small arms, predominantly rifles, and seldom at point-blank range, accuracy counted. Besides, the Austrian rifle-muskets were four inches shorter, and weighed a pound less. Even though Austrian rifles were considered inferior to Springfields or British Enfields, Partridge considers them a good gun. They were certainly an improvement over smoothbores.[19]

For the first time, Partridge states that he wishes the war were over. It is not the risk which bothers him, but the wait, and the close quarters. Early in March, the Army of the Potomac was reorganized, adding another level of command, the army Corps. The Army of the Potomac was then composed of corps, divisions, brigades, regiments, and companies. General McDowell was promoted to command the First Corps, consisting of three divisions. General King was promoted to Division Commander, replacing McDowell, and Colonel Lysander Cutler of the Sixth Wisconsin became temporary commander of King's Brigade.

On March 10th, the army did start moving. They marched some 18 miles west to Centreville. The Confederates had left, and had burned the stores they couldn't carry. On the 16th, the army returned to Arlington Heights. McClellan was then sent toward Richmond with most of the army, starting the Peninsular Campaign, but the First Corps was detached from McClellan's command and left in northern Virginia in defense of the Capitol. The Corps headquarters were to be on the Rappahannock. From there, McDowell could rejoin McClellan when and if needed. On April 4th, McDowell started toward Fredericksburg.

---

[19] Earl J. Coates and Dean S. Thomas, *An Introduction to Civil War Small Arms* (Gettysburg: Thomas Publications, 1990), pp. 9, 21. I am indebted to the historian James R. H. Spears of Indianapolis, Indiana, for a number of these observations on altered Springfield smoothbores and Austrian rifle-muskets.

FREDERICKSBURG — BUILDING BRIDGES

9.   Cordelia Howe and Phebe Holdridge   (Waukegan)

Camp near Catletts Station Va
Apr 20 1862

*Dear Sisters   it has been some time since I receaved your letter
but I guess you will excuse me when you hear the reason   in the
first place we have had some short marches   nothing of any account transpired   only that it snowd two days after we got out
here or a little back of here in the pine bushes and it was wet and
nasty..*

*we are now campt about 12 or 14 miles beyond manasses
have a very pretty camp ground and plenty [of] wood and [we
are] close by the railroad   there has been a bridge built since we
came here.   we are on the Orange and Alexandria rail road and
I expect we will have to follow it down to Richmond   the Devil
only knows when or where we will go and he wont tell.   I think
though that we will move befor many days some where..*

*there has been a report that there was a little skirmish about
twelve miles from here but I dont know as it is true   I did not
hear the particulars..   there has been a great Battle in Tenn and I
wish you would tell me wether there was any killd that went from
your place or not for I see in the list that there was a great many
Ill Regts in the fight..   we are expecting to have a great battle at
york town before long   after that is taken Richmond will have to
come I think and I dont care how quick it is done..   there is some
large farms out here   some fields are sowd to grain and it looks
very fine   I was talking to one old farmer a few days ago   he has
over 400 acres all in one peace.   he has only one male slave now.
the rebels carried away the rest of them   he said he was born and
brought up in Virginia and never had been out of the state   he
was a man about 60 years old or more..   well since the snow
storm I spoke of was over we have had fine warm weather until
today   it has raind most all day   you can guess how pleasant to
stand in the rain or ly down in a small tent*

I had a letter from home a few days ago   all well there   also one from Erie a short time ago   all well there.. well I dont think of much more to write this time   I dont see much as we have to be in camp every two hours for roll call   if we miss roll call we have to carry a loaded knapsack for two hours   I notice I only had to do so one day   well give my best respects to Hatty and all the rest of your friends &c

> *from your Brother in the army*

> *Geo W Partridge*
> *to his Sisters C S Howe &*
> *E P Holdridge*

direct as before Co G 7th Regt Wis Vol Washington D.C.

The bridge Partridge refers to is on the railroad, and presumably he has helped to build that bridge since his brigade has been assigned to work on the railroad. The skirmish he refers to was probably General Augur's Brigade, part of King's Division, pushing the small Confederate garrison out of Falmouth, on the north side of the Rappahannock opposite Fredericksburg. Before leaving, the Confederates burned the two bridges across the Rappahannock leading to the city. The great Battle in Tenn is Shiloh, where Grant secured western Tennessee for the North.

A 400 acre farm is a large one to Partridge, who knows the small subsistence farming along Lake Erie, around Waukegan, and in north central Wisconsin. To stay in one place all one's life, to farm 400 acres, to employ slaves—all this is new to Partridge. He reports it because he knows it will be novel to his sisters, too.

Hatty is a 13 year-old in Phebe Holdridge's care, probably born in Erie. She is her illegitimate or adopted daughter.

10.   Phebe Holdridge and Cordelia Howe   (Waukegan)

Camp in the woods
6 miles beyond Fredrecksburg
May 26th 1862

Dear Sisters   yours of the 18th arived here yesterday and found us all well and ready for a march   I should have answered it then but I had only got through reading it when the orders came for us to pack up for a march   we were camped then on the bank of the Rappahannock opposite Fredricksburgh   started from there at one o'clock and marched 6 miles   I dont know wether we drove the rebbels [out] or not but they have all left and we are campd on their camping ground   I heard they left last friday but their Pickets left the morning before we started   it was a hot day for marching.   the thermometer stood at 80 degrees in the shade   I saw it myself.   but we did not go very fast..

I dont think we will see much fight before we get to Richmond and dont know as we will there   but I think it will be ours before another month passes by.   well I suppose you want to know what we have been doing   we have been building bridges.   this Brigade has built three railroad bridges and have got another one to build   the largest one is acrost the Rappahannock   it is about 60 feet high and I dont know how long it is..   the other one is out beyond us a mile   the timber is all framed and will be brought here on the cars

yesterday as we were come along there was a man on a horse rode along with the brigade for a mile or more and was very inquisitive as to how large an army we had here and when we stopt to rest he left and went of into the field   that was the last I saw of him until this morning   they have got him under a guard as a Spy   they say he tryed to get ahead of the brigade and the cavalry men stopt him..   I have just heard that there has been 6 rebbel guns found close by in the brush all loaded   that shows that they left in a hurry.   well I dont think of much more news to write so I will write a little in answer to your letter

well in the first place the likeness came through all safe and very glad to get it   and that war news   I think that is the hardest treatment I ever heard of but I think it is all true from what little I have heard.   when you get some good news send it along   I do not get the papers so often now as I used to..   you wanted to know what General I was under   this part of the army is called the department of the Rappahannock under the command of Maj Genr McDowel   Genr King Commands the Division that I am in   Genr Gibbon commands the Brigade   well I will have to get another sheat

this Brigade is composed of the 6th 7th & 2nd Wisconsin and the 19th Ind   the Colonel that I enlisted under is not here   he resigned last fall..

there is a little news that I had forgot..   there was a great explosion in the city of Fredricksburgh yesterday before we left   it was the arsenal blowd up   it jard the ground over where we were

well I dont think of any more to write this time   I hope you will not delay as long as I did   I will try and not do it again   I dont know what I done it for then

best respects to all your friends   tell Hattie she must write a good long letter some day

From your only Brother in the army

  G. W. Partridge

to his sisters E. P. Holdridge & C. S. Howe

McDowell's army, officially detached from the Army of the Potomac, and now named the Department of the Rappahannock, has been camped for a month at Falmouth, opposite Fredericksburg. McDowell has been ordered to join McClellan, and the Department of the Rappahannock has started south from Fredericksburg. Partridge is excited, and looking forward, at long last, to joining the fight. He even forgets to tell his sisters about President Lincoln's visit on Friday, May 23rd, when he reviewed the troops.

There has been another change in command, and one which will have a profound effect on the Western Brigade. Brigadier General John Gibbon has been appointed commander of the Brigade. He is a regular army man, and has been in charge of Battery B of the Fourth U.S. Artillery, which has been attached to the Brigade from the early days in Arlington. At least a third of the men in the Battery have been recruited personally by Gibbon from the Brigade.[20] Gibbon is an 1847 graduate of West Point, appointed from North Carolina, but a staunch Union man. He is a stickler for discipline and drill, and wants to make his Brigade the best in the Army. He issues new uniforms to the Brigade, and with them the famous black hats, which become the fearsome identification of the Iron Brigade. They also get new dark blue frock coats with light blue trim on collars and cuffs (not unusual to the Brigade—Partridge is wearing one in his January tintype), light blue trousers (also in the tintype), white leggings, and white gloves for parade.

Nolan relates several examples of Gibbon's style of command from Gibbon's own *Personal Recollections of the Civil War* which sound like current management theory. Overhearing two soldiers say he was only an artillery officer and could not be expected to lead drill, he immediately got a book and learned how. Finding his own officers, whom he much admired, did not get up for reveille, he quickly ordered them to do so. He found that rewards for achievement got results, and that the most effective penalties were ones which hurt pride.[21] He recognized the strong spirit of these Western pioneers, and saw that it could be directed to make first-class soldiers. The great pride and unified fighting spirit Gibbon engendered in his Brigade made for very effective soldiers, essential for winning battles, but, as it would prove, at a great personal price to these young men: the percentage of Iron Brigade soldiers killed in the war would exceed that of any other Federal brigade.[22]

---

[20] Nolan, p. 40.

[21] *Ibid.*, p. 52.

[22] *Ibid.*, p. 282.

John Gibbon is not at fault. He is doing the best he can. He is one of these young men, and fights among them, and fortunately survives.

11.   Cordelia Howe and Phebe Holdridge   (Waukegan)

Camp opposite Fredricksburg
June 23 1862

Dear Sisters
*yours of the 17th reached here yesterday and found us all well
and I hope these few lines will find you the same   you may think
because we are [here] now that we have not done anything   but
not so.*

*I do not know the time we started from here but it was about
the time Banks had the fight and got drove back.   we left here on
friday about noon..   Sunday before noon we were at Catlets Station..   stopt there until tuesday when we left there for haymarket
distant 12m   Stopt there until friday when we started for Warrenton   distant 14m   Stopt there until sunday when we started
for the old Camp on the Rappahannock   arrived here wednesday
I think it raind most every day that we marchd..   I think all that
this part of the army is good for is for a show.   we have had two
reviews since we came back here..   I dont think we will ever do
any more good than we did when we went up to Warrenton.
haymarket is a station on the railroad.   there is only a few houses
but Warrenton is, as they call it here, a (rite smart) place.   it is
not a very large place but it is as large as most any of the places in
in the state..*

*they are puting on to much style in this Brigade to suit my
mind..   they want every man to carry an extra pair of pants and
shoes and coat   some of the Regts got them before they left here
and threw them away on the road   this regt did not get any   if
they had it would have been thrown away   we have enough load
to carry that we need without carrying anything extra.   I will tell
you the load I carry and I guess it is as much as any of them carrys..*

*I have in my knapsack a woolen blanket a india rubber blan-
ket half of a tent one shirt and one pair of socks.   then I have a*

haversack with two or three days rations of meat and crackers then the cartridge box with 50 rounds of cartridges and a canteen full of water   that is load enough for any man to carry.   I will never carry any more than that I dont believe   if I do I will not march far without resting and there is a good many others in the same fix..

I heard a few days ago that McDowell got throwd from his horse and got hurt some   I think some times it is a pitty he did not breake his neck or some thing worse..

I went to meting twice yesterday   you may think I am getting religous but I dont think so   in the fore noon I went over to the city   the first time I have been in a church since I left Waukegan. except once   that was at grand rappids

well a little in answer to your letter..   there was part of McDowell army in the fight but not this part..   we are expecting to hear of the great battle at Richmond every day   they have had several small fights there.   I wish I was down there to help them for I know they need all they can get and I cant see what good this division is doing here   there is two other brigades here besides this Division..   Col Me[?]alegan²³ Irish Brigade has been in a fight before Richmond   I did not know where it was from..

I sent 20 Dollars home last pay day   I dont remember what I said about Janes pay now but wait now until next pay day...

if either of you can get any postage stamps I wish you would get a dollars worth and send them to me   I have not got but one and cant get any   if you will send them the next time you write I will send you a five dollar treasury note next pay day.   the stamps are not very plenty here   all that gets them sends to Washington for them.   well I dont think of any more to write this time so good by
C. S. Howe & E. P. Holdridge
as ever your Brother in the army   G. W. Partridge

---

²³ Possibly Brig. Gen. Thomas F. Meagher.

Ps   the weather is warm and dry   it looks like rain today
some
G.W.P.
write as soon as you get this and send the stamps if possible
G. W. P.

Just a few days after Partridge's euphoria in his May 26th letter at setting out for Richmond, McDowell's Army is recalled. Partridge is discouraged. He is bitterly disappointed at turning back. He realizes that McClellan's efforts to take Richmond have been slow and not very effective. He wants to contribute. The march to Catlett's Station, Haymarket, and Warrenton, which he relates, is in full gear, in hot weather, and at a pace the men cannot keep. It is unlikely that Partridge knows what the purpose is. Whether he knows the purpose or not, he knows the army is not being very useful.

McDowell's Army, on orders from Washington, is trying to catch Stonewall Jackson, who has been conducting a harassing campaign against General Banks' Department of the Shenandoah to keep McDowell from reinforcing McClellan. Jackson escapes up the Shenandoah Valley, and McDowell marches back to Falmouth, to the camp opposite Fredericksburg. Partridge berates the Department of the Rappahannock and his Brigade as good only for show. He mocks the fine new uniforms, some parts of which some Brigade soldiers have discarded on the hot and muggy marches. There have been hundreds of stragglers. He describes his normal load on the march, some 60 pounds of equipment, and declares he will carry no more, and if forced to, he will also straggle like the others. All this must have been disappointing to Gibbon as well. Partridge blames McDowell, who is not popular.

Partridge is not pious. This seems to be true of many of the pioneers in the post-Revolution migrations. There were few churches built in Northeastern Ohio in the earliest Connecticut settlements of the Western Reserve. There were many barns built. Methodist missionaries were sent from New England in the 1840's, so the story goes, to convert a populace which could not clear a field nor raise a barn without whiskey.[24] Partridge goes to meeting (June 23rd is a Sunday) because it is the only way he can escape camp and get to the city of Fredericksburg, but assures his sisters that he is not getting religious.

---

[24] I have heard these tales from Mark Sperry, veteran lawyer, lecturer, story-teller of Chardon, Ohio, whose ancestors were settlers in Geauga County in the early 1800's.

12.   Cordelia Howe and Phebe Holdridge   (Waukegan)

Camp opposite Fredricksburg Va.
July 20 1862

Dear Sisters
your kind letters of the sixth got here a few days ago and I did not answer it rite away for reason which you shal know.   yours found us all enjoying good health and I hope these few lines will find you the same.   the reason I did not answer your letter before is because I thought I would wait until after payday.   but I changed my mind   I expect we will get our pay in a few days but dont know if we do I will send you the money as quick as I get it..

I suppose you have heard before this time that Maj General Pope has taken command of this part of the army   if not you now know it   I think he is a very good General..   here is some of the orders he has issued   this army shal get their provision through the country where they go..   also if any railroads waggon roads or telegraph is distroyed the citizens for five miles around shal fix it at their own expence   also if any Guerillia parties are found running around through the country the citizens are held responsible for giving shelter or secreting any such traitors..

this is not exactly the words that were read in the orders but it is the same meaning and amounts to the same thing..   I think they are very good orders   Gen Pope has advanced his army down to Gordensville and I think he will soon be moveing on to Richmond   I am glad to hear that old McDowell has not got quite as much to say with this army..

we are having very easy times here now   we have to drille about two hours in [a] day and that is all..   the black buries are ripe now and we get a good many of them   there is lots of fruit here now but there wont be much when it gets ripe for the boys will get it all while it is green..

there was nothing going on here the fourth   only the national salute of 36 guns in the morning at noon and at eavening.

General King got about $2.00 worth of fire works for the eavening that was the best part of the day.

well a little in answer to your letters.   in the first place I was very glad to get the stamps for mine were all gone and very thankful to you for sending them   and about the money I spoke of   I have not thought of it much yet.   but I dont know how it will be as Father wants so much of the money and I want a little here myself for there is some times they do not give us enough to eat..   but I will think a little more about.

well I dont think of much more to write this time   Give my love to Hatty and all the rest of the folks.   direct as before only not to the care of Capt Stevens for he is no longer our Capt   he has resigned and gone home and we have got another one   his name is Homer Drake

Well good by for the present from your Brother in the army
        Geo. W. Partridge
        to his sisters
        C S Howe & E.P.H.

There is some satisfaction in General John Pope's taking charge of the Army. His orders concerning civilians seem for effect, and though mostly bluster, seem to provide a basis for again feeling worthy. They inflame the enemy. Gibbon himself no doubt read the orders to the Brigade. Richmond is ever the goal for ending the war, but not until Grant will this goal again come in sight. The Federal forces in Virginia and around Washington are again reorganized, this time into the Army of Virginia, with Pope as head and Frémont (soon replaced by Sigel), Banks, and McDowell as Corps Commanders.

Partridge has fallen back into the routine of camp life, with short hours, blackberries and other fruit in abundance, and fireworks on the Fourth of July. He has stopped complaining.

13.   Celia Slocum   (Erie)

Camp opposite Fredericksburg
Aug 2 1862

Dear sister   haveing not heard from you in so long a time I concluded that my last letter did not get there and so I thought I would write again.. we are all well here and I hope these few lines will find you the same.. I dont know as there is much news to write   there is not much war news around here.   it is reported that there is some rebbel forces out to Gordons Ville but how many I do not know..   I understand that our forces have possession of the city
we are going to get our pay today   they are paying part of the regement now..   the most of us do not get full pay this time as we have had a settlement with the Government.   and we have had to pay for the cloths that we got in the state which was condemed clothing when we got it and we did not half ware it out..   that is what makes the bills so large..   I get seaventeen dollars..   some get more and some less according to how much blue clothing they have had   well I dont think of much more to write this time as there is not much news in camp..   write as often as you can and you will hear from me as often as you write..   this is a short letter but I cant think of any thing to write   so good by for the present
from your Brother
George W. Partridge
to his sister C. M. Slocum

Seaven oclock P.M.
well sister I thought I would give you a little discription of the way we have got our camp fixed..   each Company has two roes of tents   between the roes is a sort of turnpike road about 12 feet wide   the tents are all covered with bushes and about ten feet in front of the tents so as to make a shade   but I think it is more for the looks than anything else as we want to see which Regt can

*have the best looking camp..   this Company has got the best
looking street in this Regt if not in the Brigade..   we have got all
our tents raised from the ground about a foot and beds made of
smal poles with brush for feathers..*

well I dont think of any more to write this time   so good night

George W Partridge

Partridge has not written to his sisters in Erie since February.
Perhaps a letter from them was lost in the mail.

With little to do, Pope has sent small parties out on intelligence
missions. Gibbon, with a small contingent drawn from his Brigade
and from Battery B, finds Jackson at Gordonsville, some 40 miles
Southwest of Fredericksburg, and estimates he has 30,000 men.
There is no engagement.

The settlement with the Government was probably deductions
from pay to cover clothing discarded on the march. Partridge wrote
in his letter of June 23rd (letter 11) that he had not thrown away any
clothing because he had not been issued any extra, but that he had
enough to carry and would not carry more. He was probably issued
more, and probably discarded it, and has been charged for it.

Fixing up the camp and making it a competition to look the best
is of course a way to cope with the boredom of camp life and make it
more bearable.

14.   Cordelia Howe and Phebe Holdridge   (Waukegan)

Camp opposite Fredericksburg
Aug 9, 1862

Dear Sisters
I will now write a few lines to you again and let you know
what we are doing down here   we got our pay over a week ago
and I will send you what I prommised you in this   I have not
heard from you since I wrote before but I thought I would write
now for we may leave here before many days...
this Brigade started out on a reconnoytering expedition last
monday   we started at one oclock in the morning..   we went out
about 17 miles before we found any of the enemy when we run on
to a small body of cavelry and some artilery..   they fired a few
shots and left..   this Regt did not get in sight of them   it was an
awful hot day and more than half of the regt had to stop on ac-
count of the heat   the regt formed a line when they got where the
battery was planted and they said there was not more than a third
of a regt there   I stopt about 80 rods behind.   we stopt there all
night   the next morning we went about 2 or 3 miles farther when
we was orderd back..   when we got back to where we hat stopt the
night before we heard the cannon fireing   it seemed the rebbels
had been trying to come in behind us and had found something
els to contend with..   this regt was the guard for the waggons   the
Battery and the other Regts went on   the artilery got there in time
to fire a few shots and the 2nd Regt fired one round   the rebbels
were fireing on a waggon train and they captured it   the train
belonged to General Augur Brigade   our captain was out with
some waggons for this brigade and he saw the hole of it   he did
not know but they would come after them but they did not..   I
dont know of but one man being shot..   they say there was some
men in the waggons that were taken...   every thing was quiet when
we got there   we stopt there over night..   the next day we went to
a place called Spotsylvania   stopt there until six oclock and

started for camp   we travelled till ten oclock that night   the next morning we came home.. I stood very well after the first day..

we have orders now to move tomorrow night for warrenton General Burnside has come in here with 60000 men   they say he has that many but I dont think he has quite as many as that   well I dont think of any more to write this time   write soon

From your Brother Geo. W. Partridge
to his sisters C. S. Howe & E. P. H.

On August 3rd, General Halleck, Grant's superior in the West, recently brought to Washington as general-in-chief to bring order and coordination to the Federal efforts in the East, ordered McClellan to abandon his Peninsular campaign and to return with his army to northern Virginia. Pope was directed to disrupt Confederate railroads and communications to prevent the Confederates from concentrating their forces on McClellan while he made the move.

Frederick's Hall Station, some 30 miles southwest of Fredericksburg, was on the railroad Lee would use from Richmond to Gordonsville, where Jackson had already moved his army from Richmond. Pope ordered Gibbon to destroy the railroad at Frederick's Hall Station. On August 5th, Gibbon started out from Fredericksburg with his Brigade and a small force of artillery and cavalry. He sent Colonel Cutler ahead with the Sixth Wisconsin, with some of the artillery and cavalry, to carry out the raid, while he took the Second and Seventh Wisconsin and the Nineteenth Indiana by another route. Some of Augur's Brigade, now under General Hatch, followed Gibbon's group.

Partridge seems unaware of the purpose of the march, and calls it a "reconnoytering expedition." They run into a small Confederate force and drive it off. It has been very hot, and Partridge misses the action, stopping 80 rods behind. The three regiments stop their march, and camp for the night on the road. Starting out again the next morning, August 6th, they are soon ordered back. Partridge hears artillery and rifle fire, and learns that the rebels have attacked and captured some of Augur's wagons, and have taken some prisoners. The action is close by, but Partridge misses it again— "everything was quiet when we got there." The next day, August 7th, they go to Spotsylvania Court House and wait there till 6:00 P.M., march till 10:00 P.M., and return to camp near Fredericksburg on the morning of August 8th.

The reason that Gibbon withdrew on August 6th was that his cavalry had spotted J.E.B. Stuart approaching from the south with a large force. Stuart came on and captured a number of wagons from Hatch's Brigade. Gibbon and Hatch stayed and skirmished, and although casualties were few, 59 stragglers were captured by Stuart, who then broke off the engagement. Gibbon waited the next day in Spotsylvania Court House for Cutler to return from his raid.

Cutler's raid on Frederick's Hall Station was a complete success, carried out with dispatch and without a casualty. In a little over three days his men had marched 91 miles in intense heat, and had destroyed two miles of railroad. Exhausted, they managed to rejoin Gibbon at Spotsylvania Court House and return with the Brigade to Falmouth.

Partridge's stopping 80 rods (a quarter of a mile) behind in the heat of the first day is the sort of straggling which led to the capture of 59 men, and illustrates the hazards of marching in woolen uniforms carrying 60-plus pounds of gear in Virginia's summer heat. The first day's march started in the middle of the night, trading sleep for a cooler march. In this brigade, especially with Gibbon, straggling is hardly willful, and probably indicates exhaustion. Partridge remarks pointedly, "I stood very well after the first day."

Burnside's arrival at Falmouth signals that the Brigade's war is about to begin.

THE IRON BRIGADE IN BATTLE — 1862

15.   Cordelia Howe and Phebe Holdridge   (Waukegan)

Camp near Sharpsburgh Maryland
Sept 20   1862

Dear Sisters

I received your letter a long time ago but have neglected to answer it until now for reasons which you shal know.. in the first place the mail does not go out very often.   I suppose you have heard of the great battle of Bull Run   I was not in much of that battle.   but we have had two more in Md both of which I came through safe..

the first one was fought on sunday night the 14 and the devils got behind a stone fence in front of our Regt   but they could not make us run   we fought until we fired all of our ammunition away and then laid down to wait for reinforcements which came about 11 oclock.. the enemy all left before morning..

there was one killed and 12 wounded in this Company..

Wednesday we had the satisfaction of seeing the curses run. part of the brigade was fighting in a cornfield and our regt came up and gave them a cross fire and they run as if they were scart.. and I presume they were some.. in the last fight we lost 2 killed and 3 wounded.. the 6 Regt and 2 Regt lost more than any of the rest.. this Regt numbers about 150. the 2 Regt does not number 100 now..

the nighest any of their shots has come to me is to tear a hole in my sleeve   if they dont come any nigher than that I wont grumble.

well I dont think of much more to write this time   it has been some time since we have had any mail   the last one I got was from Erie.. well I dont think of any more this time   you may think I am dead   but I dont think so yet

good by for the present
from your Brother
Geo. W. Partridge

> *to his sisters*
>   *C. S. Howe*
>   *and*
>   *E. P. Holdridge*
> *PS   direct as before*

In the six weeks since the previous letter a great deal has happened. Rather than attack the withdrawing McClellan, Lee has decided to take off after Pope's Army of Virginia. Stonewall Jackson, reinforced with J.E.B. Stuart's Cavalry and Longstreet's Corps, now outnumbered Pope's Army, even with the addition of a sizeable number of Burnside's men. Pope was no longer the hunter, but the hunted. He retreated across the Rappahannock below Bull Run, and waited for reinforcements from McClellan. Pope now faced a 55,000-man Confederate force across the Rappahannock, but was soon joined by 30,000 men returning from the Army of the Potomac, bringing his force to 75,000. On August 25th, Jackson, with 25,000 men, made an end-run to the west, then northward, then eastward, and got behind Pope's army, destroying Pope's stores.

Reasoning that the rest of Lee's army would follow Jackson, Pope moved to block the way, and to catch Jackson's smaller force, now at Manassas. On August 27th, Jackson moved quickly to the north and hid in an abandoned railway cut north of the Warrenton Pike, east of Gainesville, near the First Bull Run battlefield of the previous year. Jackson heard there that Longstreet was on the way to join him, so when King's Division came marching by, looking for Jackson, who King thought was far ahead to the east, Jackson opened fire with his artillery, 25,000 men against King's 10,000.

Gibbon's Brigade, 2,100 strong, was directly in line along the road. It was already early evening, past six o'clock. Gibbon placed his one battery, Battery B, to the right, to answer the Confederate artillery, and the two sides converged to within 75 yards, with virtually no cover. Two other regiments of King's Division rushed up and joined the fight, bringing the Federal engagement to 2,900 men. Directly opposite were 6,400 of Jackson's men with many more in reserve. The fight went on until dark, when both sides stopped shooting. With no Federal help coming, King's Division left in the night for Manassas. Gibbon's Brigade had lost 133 killed, 539 wounded, and 79 missing, 751 casualties in all, 36% of the effective strength of the brigade. Total Federal casualties were 912 of 2,900 men engaged. It was the first major encounter for the Western Brigade, and they had fought bravely, without flinching. Gibbon's drilling and tough training had prepared them well. The Brigade lost seven of twelve officers, including Colonel Robinson of the Seventh Wisconsin. He would recover. Jackson lost 2,200 killed and wounded of the 6,400 engaged, his largest percentage losses in the war. Jackson's men would remember the black-hatted soldiers.

The battle on August 28th became known as the Battle of Gainesville. Nolan calls it the Battle at Brawner Farm, a more appropriate name, since Gainesville was some distance away, and part of the theater of the Second Battle of Bull Run on August 29th and 30th. Gibbon's Brigade, the Black Hat Brigade, had a less central rôle in the Second Bull Run battle, but suffered an additional 144 casualties, bringing total casualties for the three days to nearly 900. Total Federal casualties for the three days were nearly 14,000, including nearly 4,000 missing and probably captured; Confederate casualties were 8,400 killed and wounded. The Federal armies regrouped in Centreville, and returned to camp again near Washington, where they had started from back in March.

It is curious that Partridge, in referring to the battle at Bull Run, states, "I was not in much of that battle." It is true that on August 29th and 30th the Seventh Wisconsin's involvement was small overall, but he does not even mention Gainesville here. Perhaps, for some reason not apparent in the letters, he was not in the action then. There is no mention of his being sick or wounded in his letters. It is also probable that the engagements on August 28th, 29th, and 30th were considered one battle at the time, and that it was only some time later that Gainesville became known as a battle in its own right. I think it is also likely that he is saturated with the impressions and scope of the previous week's fighting. He is camped near the Antietam battlefield, and is probably engaged in clean-up and burial details there. The Battle of Antietam dwarfed all previous Civil War

Battles, and had the highest single-day casualties of any battle in American history, before or since. Partridge does not like to talk about himself, even when pressed by his sisters. He is suddenly older. He is serious, stark in his reporting, and his humor, if that is what it is, contains an irony that stops laughter.

After Second Bull Run, the Army of Virginia was merged back into the Army of the Potomac under McClellan. Pope was relieved and sent to the Northwest. McDowell was replaced as Commander of the First Corps by Major General Joseph Hooker. General King, who was not well at Gainesville, was replaced as Commander of the First Division by General Hatch. Gibbon's Brigade and those of Phelps, Doubleday, and Patrick made up the First Division.

With little delay, the Army of the Potomac took off after Lee on September 6th. McClellan, by good fortune, found a memo from Lee outlining the proposed Confederate plan to invade Maryland. Longstreet was to go with half of Lee's force to secure Boonsborough and Hagerstown. The balance of the army would proceed to Harper's Ferry, a large Federal arsenal, and take it and the heights above it on both sides of the Potomac. The army would then reassemble at Boonsborough and Hagerstown. McClellan hurried to meet Lee's reduced force at Boonsborough before the rest of Lee's army could get there. By September 13th, McClellan was in Frederick, Maryland, where Lee had been a few days before. From Frederick, on the morning of September 14th, McClellan marched over Catoctin Mountain and into the long valley running north and south between Catoctin Mountain and South Mountain. There were several gaps over South Mountain, and the Confederates had these well defended. Gibbon's Brigade marched the six miles across the valley, through Middletown. Having by chance led the way at Gainesville, Gibbon's Brigade was now assigned the task of leading the way up the National Road over South Mountain against the strong defenses there. Gibbon wanted his men to perform well, since the whole Army of the Potomac would now be watching.[25]

---

[25] Nolan, p. 121.

Well up the mountain they met some artillery fire, and heavy rifle fire, and charged up anyway, suffering many casualties. The Seventh Wisconsin was on the right side of the road, the north side, and was stopped finally at a stone wall, heavily defended. It got dark, but the firing continued.

Partridge describes the fight here, and will again later in more detail. He demonizes the enemy, as soldiers usually do. It is significant to Partridge that the enemy could not make them run. The shame of the disorganized retreat at the First Battle of Bull Run, a year earlier, in which the Second Wisconsin participated, sticks with this Brigade. Never again would they panic. It is very important to stand one's ground. Partridge's report of 13 casualties in Company G is nearly proportional to the total Seventh Regiment's 147 casualties in its 10 companies, the highest loss by far among the four regiments in the brigade in this engagement, but fewer than the 240-odd Seventh Regiment casualties at Gainesville.

At South Mountain, Gibbon's Brigade received from General Hooker the name that stuck with them for the rest of the war—the Iron Brigade. The men liked their new name, and their reputation grew.[26]

Across South Mountain, Lee, with 18,000 men, had turned southwest at Boonsborough towards Sharpsburg, eight miles away. The Army of the Potomac followed. On Monday night, September 15th, Hooker, with his First Corps, stopped and made camp north of Sharpsburg on the east side of the Hagerstown Turnpike. McClellan did nothing all day the 16th, squandering his advantage as Confederate forces continued to arrive from Hagerstown and from the Harper's Ferry area. By Wednesday, Lee would have 50,000 men to McClellan's 75,000. The Iron Brigade was up very early on Wednesday, the 17th, and leading the way again, made their way south on the Hagerstown Turnpike toward Sharpsburg. They were met by artillery fire and deadly fire from sharpshooters. They ran into Jackson again full force at 6:00 A.M. The Second and Sixth Wisconsin were on the left side of the road, the east side, and the

---

[26] *Ibid.*, p. 130. See also note 50, p. 335ff.

Seventh Wisconsin and the Nineteenth Indiana were on the right. Ahead of the Second and Sixth was a cornfield of perhaps 30 acres, taller than a man's head. It was full of Confederate soldiers, their bayonets glistening in the morning sun above the corn. Battery B was brought up on the right of the cornfield, and fired into it.[27] The Second and Sixth Wisconsin also fired into it and charged through it and over a fence, rushing onward toward their objective of the Dunker Church, a small whitewashed building on a small rise to the west of the Turnpike. The Confederates rallied, and with reinforcements, pushed the two regiments back to the cornfield fence. This is when the Seventh Wisconsin and the Nineteenth Indiana turned to their left and caught the advancing Confederates in a crossfire. There is a slight depression on the west side of the Turnpike here, and coming up out of it toward the Turnpike, the Seventh and Nineteenth appeared suddenly upon the side of the Confederates and surprised them, and had the satisfaction of seeing them run. They had not seen that before. Fresh Confederate troops under Law and Hood came up from the south and drove the Brigade back toward their Battery. The Confederates brought more men to bear on the right of the Brigade, and tried to take the Battery. The brigade rallied around their Battery and held them off, and as fresh Union troops swept in front of them from their left, they limbered up the Battery to the remaining horses and withdrew to their camp up the Turnpike. It was not yet 8:00 A.M., but the Brigade was through for the day.[28] There was little left of it. They had set out before 6:00 A.M.

---

[27] R. V. Johnson and C. C. Buel, editors, *Battles and Leaders of the Civil War* (New York: Castle Books, 1956), Vol. II, p. 639, note, General Hooker's report. Hooker observed the battle at the cornfield, and was wounded there.

[28] The Carman-Cope *Atlas of the Battlefield of Antietam*, 1904, available from the National Archives, and also available for view at the Antietam National Battlefield, maps 1-6. These show the position on the battlefield of all combatants, including the regiments of the Iron Brigade (Gibbon) and Battery B (Campbell) at 1) Daybreak, 2) 6:00-6:20 A.M., 3) 6:45-7:00 A.M., 4) 7:20 A.M., 5) 7:30 A.M., and 6) 8:00 A.M. There are 14 maps for the day. The Iron Brigade is engaged only in maps 2-5. The maps were compiled from a survey mailed in the 1880's to hundreds of veterans of the battle, North and South, asking them what they did on the battlefield, where they did it, and exactly when they did it.

with 800 men. There were 343 killed and wounded, and 5 missing, leaving some 450.

Partridge considers himself lucky with only a bullet hole torn in his sleeve. He does not think he is dead yet, but he is wondering why he isn't. He has been thinking out loud about it.

Results were averaged for each regiment, and the averages plotted on the maps. The maps look plausible, but may not be statistically reliable.

THE UNION
AND THE
CONSTITUTION

Arlington hights O 3 1861
Dear sister Doubtless you have heard
that I was in the army before
this time well I am here
I enlisted in a company a Grand
Rapids some time in awgust I stayd
there about two weeks and went
to madison stayed on the camp
ground there about a month and
drilled I did not go into the
city while I stayd there well
we started from there about ten
o'clock on saturday I have forgot
what day of the month it was
but we came by the way of Janes
-ville to Chicago arrived in
Chicago about eight P. M.

16.   Celia Slocum   (Erie)

Camp some where in Maryland
Sept 21 1862

Dear sister   it has been some time since I received your letter   I neglected to answer it until now for several reasons..   in the first place the mail does not go from here very often and we have been marching most of the time..   I have not written a letter since I left Ceder mountain until yesterday..

I suppose you have heard some of the battles we have had. the Brigade has been in four fights   I was not with them in the first one but fave [have?] been in all the rest..   and I dont care about going in any more..   the Brigade is very badly cut up.   I dont think there is over 450 in it fit for duty   there is 150 in this Regt and it is larger than the others..

the first fight in Md was on sunday night 14   it commenced about 6 oclock P M and lasted about four hours   in the morning the devils were all gone.   we lost from our Company one killed 12 wounded   at bull run we lost 3 killed 6 wounded and 7 taken prisoners.

the fight on the 17th commenced early in the morning and lasted all day.   we went in, in the morning and gave them them a cross fire and made them run but they would not stay run but came back to try it over and we were ordered back..   we lost 2 killed 2 wounded..

the numbr I have mentioned is out of this Company.   the rebels all left where where the fight was the 17.   left in the night and went to the river and I dont know but they have crossed before this time   I fired over 50 rounds of ammunition the first night..   well I dont think of much more to write this time..   I forget to give you the directions every time but have not forgot it this time direct to

    Company G 7 Regt
    Wisconsin Volenteers

Washington D.C.
well good by for the present   write soon
from your Brother
       G W Partridge
       C. M. Slocum

This is written only a day after the the letter to Cordelia Howe and Phebe Holdridge, but its tone is different, more sober. Celia Slocum, after all, has always been grown up to Partridge, more mother than sister. No bravado here, no tale of a bullet's near miss, no ironic contemplation of his death. Partridge states that the Brigade has been in four fights. He may be including the First Battle of Bull Run on July 21, 1861, among these, which only the Second Wisconsin had been in, before the present brigade was formed. The three fights Partridge *has* been in are Gainesville-Second Bull Run, South Mountain, and Antietam. Partridge had been eager to go into battle. Now he doesn't "care about going in any more." He can tell Celia Slocum "the the Brigade is very badly cut up." He would not tell Cordelia Howe that. "I don't think there is over 450 in it fit for duty" is exactly on the mark. His casualty numbers, he states twice, are for his Company. 150 fit for duty in his Regiment is a far cry from the 1,106 who entrained from Madison a year ago. He doesn't tell Celia Slocum of his "satisfaction of seeing the curses run." He can share that with his comrades and with his kid-sister. He did not tell his kid-sister that "they would not stay run but came back to try it over and we were ordered back."[29] He does not have to impress Celia Slocum. She is twelve years his senior; he feels no rivalry with her.

Partridge is writing better now. He has had some practice, of course, through writing letters, and through reading them. But he is also more expressive now, more concentrated.

Troop strength and battlefield losses seem to have an elusive and elastic quality. Enemy troop strength is always greater than ours,

---

[29] This seems to substantiate an early withdrawal from the fight, in agreement with the Carman-Cope maps, in note 28, above.

while enemy losses are very large, and unsustainable. We shouldn't have these distortions, however, on estimates of our own side's strength and loss. Until the draft, or until after Gettysburg, losses in companies, and even in regiments, were seldom made up through new recruits. The regiments simply got smaller and smaller. Average Union regimental strength at Gettysburg was 375, down from 1,000 or so; average company strength was 32, down from 100.[30] New recruits more often formed new regiments. But wounded and missing account for some natural elasticity. Partridge writes of 450 fit for duty. "Wounded" is the largest category of casualties. Some 15% of the wounded die from those wounds.[31] There was no conception of microbial causes of infection or of disease in the 1860's, and certainly no antibiotics. A sizeable number of wounded recover, and are discharged for disability. But perhaps 50% or more of the wounded return to duty, and some after considerable lengths of time. So of the 626 wounded at Gainesville-Second Bull Run some 300-plus might return, and of the total Iron Brigade wounded from Gainesville through Antietam, from August 28th through September 17th, some 1,150 men, 500 to 600 might eventually return.

"Missing" can be stragglers or lost soldiers who may turn up. Or they may be wounded and in the care of another unit. Or they may be prisoners who escape or are exchanged. In all of these instances and categories there are current errors, and over time, loss of records.

[30] Boatner, p. 612.

[31] John W. Busey, *These Honored Dead: The Union Casualties at Gettysburg* (Hightstown, NJ: Longstreet House, 1988), p. 6.

17.   Phebe Holdridge and Cordelia Howe   (Waukegan)

Camp near Bakersville
Oct 23/62

Dear sisters   yours of the 15th came along here yesterday and you may be sure I was glad to hear from you again and hear that you enjoyed good health   we are all well here   what there is left of us..

well you want to know wether I took aim at any particular Rebbel or not.   I took aim at one several times but they always fell before I could fire.   some times when I would get a good aim at one rebbel there would be another rebbel come up before him so I could not hit the one that I aimed at.   but to tell the truth I could not tell wether I killed any or not as they fell so fast..   but I know I tryed as hard as I could to kill some of them.

well it is geting late and cold and I guess I will quit for tonight and finish in the morning..

Oct 24

well good morning to you all   this is a fine morning but cold. well now I will try and finish..

you want to know how I like the idea of so many bullets flying around me.   well for my part I would rather be a little farther away from them..   some may like to hear the music they make but I dont..   at the battle of South mountain I could not see any one to aim at as it was dark before we commenced   but I aimed at the fire from their guns and I guess that was close to them..   we all done the best we could that night   I fired about 70 times at them and that was all I had..   at the battle of Antietam we did not fire so many times for there was another Regt came to relieve us..

I dont know what you would think but I thought we were in a dangerous place when we laid down and the cannon ball and shell were flying over us thick and fast.   and it seemed as though

every one was going to hit some one in the regt.. I did not feel
scart nor excited when I was fireing at them.   I thought of nothing els but load and fire as fast as I could   but to ly down and
have nothing to think of but them shells whistleing over us I felt as
though I wanted to crowd into the earth... but when we were
fighting the boys would laugh to see them tumble and fall.   you
might think that we coild not sleep when we were in so much
danger but not so   for at the battle of south mountain after we
had fired all of our ammunition away we laid down and I guess
half the Regt was asleep before the reinforcements came   I know
I was any way   well to say the best of it it is dangerous work and
I would rather be out of it..

   well as to the food we have to eat it is something of a variety
we have crackers fresh beef and coffee for breakfast.   and fresh
beef crackers and coffee for dinner   and for supper we have coffee
crackers and fresh beef..   about once a week we get a small ration
of pork and beens.   that is the amount of our provision and no
money to buy any thing with..   you want to know what General
we are under..   before the fight we were under Maj General
Hooker but now he is wounded I dont know who commands the
corpse   but we are under McClellan now..

   we have plenty of clothing except shirts.   I have got one or
part of one

      now I am going to ask one favor of you.   I want you to send
me 2 3 or 4 dollars if you can for I want to get a few things and
have no money to buy with   it has been most 4 months since we
got our pay and I guess we wont get it until the 4 months is up
and if you will send me that I will send you some back when we
get our pay.   if you cant send the money send one dollars worth
of postage stamps for I am out now   I want you to write as soon
as you get this and not wait one day.   I am not so particular with
every one..   well I dont think of any more news this time..   there
is no sign of us leaving here very soon and I guess I will close
hopeing these few lines will find you enjoying good health.   direct
as before..

I remain as ever your affectionate Brother
George W. Partridge jr
E. P. Holdridge. &. C. S. Howe
P. S.   the weather is cold to be outdoors as we have to   we have
the small tents but they dont keep out the wind much
G W Partridge

Oct 28/62

Camp near Bakersville

Dear sisters yours of the 15th
came along here yesterday and
you may be sure I was glad
to hear from you again
one [...] that you [...]
good health we are all well
here what there is left
of us   well you want
to know wether I took aim
at any particular Rebbel
or not. I took aim at one
several times but they always
fell before I could fire.
some times when I would get
a good aim at one rebbel there
would be another rebbel
come up before him so I
could not hit the one that
I aimed at. but to tell
the truth I could not tell
wether I killed any or not

... but I aimed at the fire
from their guns and I guess
that was close to them — we all
done the best we could that
night. I fired about 70 times
at them and that was all
I had — at the battle of
Antietam we did not fire so
many times for there was
another Regt came to relieve us.
I dont know what you will
think but I thought we were
in a dengerous place when
we laid down and the common
ball and shell were flyin
over us thick and fast
and it seemed as though every
one was going to hit some one
in the regt. I did not
feel scart nor excited when
I was fireing at them.
I thought of nothing els but
... fire at ... I wild

The Army of the Potomac is still in Maryland, a little north of Sharpsburg and the Antietam battlefield. Soon they will be moving south. Partridge writes nothing about Lincoln's visit to Antietam, nor about the Emancipation Proclamation which was announced September 22nd, to become effective January 1st. Nor does he say anything about the new Western regiment which joined the depleted Brigade on October 8th, the Twenty-fourth Michigan Volunteers, recruited in the Detroit area. They were green troops, and were not yet issued black hats. It was felt that they must earn them. The veterans of the Brigade were cool to them, partly because they were green, and partly because they were so eager for battle. The veterans no longer had that eagerness, though they would continue to fight with the pride of the Iron Brigade.

Although Partridge seems in better spirits here than he was immediately after the South Mountain and Antietam battles, he has reflected on his experiences in battle and would rather be out of it. In his opening greeting he listens to his habitual "we are all well here," and adds, with some irony, "what there is left of us."

His sister's question about aiming at a particular rebel is probably an ethical one. It personalizes the enemy by directing attention to an individual, and by making Partridge responsible for killing a person, when Partridge has been generalizing about them as devils. He doesn't brag about killing the devils, and dodges specific responsibility. But he weighs and answers the ethical question. He is, after all, a volunteer. He is defending his country, himself, and, most of all, his friends around him. Lee, arguing with Longstreet at the point of woods at Gettysburg, points across to Cemetery Ridge and declares, "The enemy is there, General Longstreet, and I am going to strike him."[32] Partridge, at *his* scale, says the same. The enemy is there, and he is going to shoot him, and *knows* he tries as hard as he can to kill some of them.

Answering a more general question from his sister about what it feels like to be in battle, he says he doesn't like the bullets flying

[32] Arthur Crew Inman, editor, *Soldier of the South*, George Pickett, Letters (Boston: 1928), p. 56.

around him. He even jokes about it. But in such a situation, as in the dark at South Mountain, you stand your ground and do what you can to respond to those flying bullets: "we all did the best we could that night   I fired about 70 times at them and that was all I had."[33]

Being shelled is different. You know the danger and are frightened because you and your comrades are the only targets. While firing, Partridge is not scared nor excited. He thinks only of loading and firing as fast as he can. Then he is on a team, one of the boys in the game who would "laugh to see them tumble and fall." I have seen grown men shoot down the video Space Invaders, and laugh to see them tumble and fall. "but to ly down and have nothing to think of but them shells whistleing over us I felt as though I wanted to crowd into the earth..."—that is the unreasoned terror of battle. And then this repose, even in danger, when he had done the best he could and could do no more, tired from marching all day, from charging up a mountain, pinned down in a field by the enemy behind a stone wall, dead and wounded comrades all around, exhausted and in the dark: "for at the battle of south mountain after we fired all of our ammunition away we laid down and I guess half the Regt was asleep before the reinforcements came   I know I was any way."

This whole passage has the ring of *The Red Badge of Courage*. Stephen Crane, who was in no war, must have heard such accounts from soldiers like George Partridge.

Partridge lightens up, and tells the soldiers' perennial joke about the variety in his meals. He is out of money again (because he has not been paid in nearly four months), and can't buy anything from the sutlers, the entrepreneurial merchants who set up shop in the camps. He is also out of postage stamps, as he often is. He asks his sisters to send him money or stamps, "and not to wait one day." Endearingly, he adds he "is not so particular with every one."

---

[33]Partridge goes on to say that he didn't fire so many times at Antietam because they were relieved, corroborating again the short engagement.

18.   Cordelia Howe and Phebe Holdridge   (Waukegan)

Camp near Brooks Station
Nov 28, 1862

Dear Sisters
    Once more I take my pen in hand to answer your letter.   it has been some time since I receaved it but could not answer it for I had no writing material nor stamps.   but our Lieut. got some stamps and I got a few from him and got trusted for them and I have borrowd some paper so I guess I can make it go.
    since I wrote to you before we have had some marching to do and here we are about 8 miles from Fredericksburgh and about the same distance from Aquia Creek and a half mile from the station.
    we have had good weather most of the time.   it raind two days while we were on the march   that made the roads bad, but it has dried up a great deal since..
    th Rebbels still hold Fredericksburgh.   I dont know how soon we may have to go and drive them out of it but the sooner the better for me   the railroad is finished as far as here.   I guess as soon as they can get it done any farther we will move.
    I guess you get more news about the war than I do   if you dont you dont get much for there is not many papers brought in here and if there was I could not buy them..   the Paymaster has not come yet.   there is some talk about his comeing this week or next but I dont know how it is nor I dont care much if they only give me plenty to eat and plenty of writing material   but that is what they wont do..   the clothing has come since I wrote before so that we have plenty of that.   the land around here is very poor. there is no very large farmes around here.   the land is all growd over with pines   that is[,] where the pines will grow.   where they wont grow there is nothing growing..   Our Colonel came back to the Regement today.   the first time he has been with us since the battle of <u>Gainsville</u>   he was wounded there and was

sick in the bargin and it took him a good while to get well.   the
whole Regt was turned out to <u>Cheer</u> him when he come and every
one Cheerd as loud as he could..
   Celia writes to me that they had a great time <u>drafting</u> there.
she said one man cut his <u>thumb</u> off to prevent his being drafted
and then had to go   I think that was quite a joke on him or his
thumb..   if you can get any stamps I wish you would send them
along and when we get paid I will send you the money for them
for I dont know when I can get any more
   I am very thankful that I dont use tobacco for it costs double
price and the boys that do use it cant get money to buy with.
well I cant think of any more to write this time so I will close by
saying give my best respects to Hatty and all the rest of the folks
   Write as often as you can and direct as before

           yours with a Brothers love
             Geo. W. Partridge. jr
           C.S. Howe & E. P. Holdridge

P. S.   tell Hatty to write a few lines the next time you write
              G . W . P .

It is again over a month since Partridge's last letter, but no further fights have occurred. The Iron Brigade has returned to Virginia,
near Fredericksburg. Lee's army this time is in Fredericksburg, and
not off defending Richmond. Partridge will prove correct that a
move toward Fredericksburg is coming.

The returning Regimental colonel is William Robinson, obviously
well-liked. The intensity of the cheering may have other roots as
well. On November 4th, General John Gibbon had been promoted
to Commander of the Second Division. Colonel Solomon Meredith
was promoted to Brigadier General and given command of the
Brigade, over the strong objections of Gibbon, who thought Meredith incompetent, and preferred Colonel Lysander Cutler. Gibbon
had strong feelings about his Brigade. Nolan quotes Gibbon, a

North Carolinian, writing after the war that "at the judgment day I want to be with Wisconsin soldiers."[34]   Also in November, General George McClellan was relieved from duty and the Army of the Potomac turned over to General Ambrose Burnside. McClellan was very popular among the soldiers. So Colonel Robinson represented a stable and familiar commander to the Seventh Wisconsin, despite the upheaval in the higher command. He was also, like Gibbon and Cutler, an officer who fought alongside his men. His wound was that badge. As an officer, and wounded, he could have easily resigned.

The long-term volunteer soldiers who knew what battle was like wished strongly for other young men to share in that experience. They heartily approved of the draft. Partridge will write further on this as shorter-term volunteers are mustered out.

---

[34] Nolan, p. 167.

19.   Cordelia Howe and Phebe Holdridge   (Waukegan)

Camp near Belle Plain
Jan 12 1863

Dear sisters

    I take this opportunity to write to you   having not heard from you in so long a time I thought I would write again and find out the reason you did not write.. Possibly the letter did not get here and it may get here yet..

    Well there is not much news to write this time. I suppose you have heard of the great battle we had here at Fredericksburgh.. I cant give much of a discription except that we went over there and came back again all right.   we were not in the fight much but were exposed to the shells a great deal and lost some men. if you could only immagine how the shells sound when they go over us I am sure I cant tell you what they sound like for I have never heard any thing sound like them before nor never want to again.. we were lying in a ditch one spell where the mud was about shoe deep and the shells were flying over us like hail stones and every one that came over I would stick my head in the mud. well that is enough of that we got back safe. we moved around some after we got back but have stopt at last down here..

    We have been putting up winter quarters here.. myself and three others have got a small shanty 6 feet by 12 and coverd it with our shelter tents but I dont know how long they will let us stay here to enjoy them

    Well a little about the weather we have had fine warm weather ever since the Battle very little rain. some frost every night.

    I had a letter from home a few days ago   all rite up there also one from erie all rite there also one from Cousin Louisa she has lost two Brothers since the war broke out and her last Brother is now in the army..

    Well I dont know as I can think of any more this time.

If you have not sent any Postage Stamps please send me a dollars worth and I will send you the money for them the next time as I have no change less than five dollars

Well good by for this time from your Brother
C. S. H. & E. P. H.   *Geo. W. Partridge jr*

Until December 9th, the Iron Brigade stayed at Brooks Station, except for the new Twenty-fourth Michigan. They patrolled the twelve miles of railroad from Aquia Creek Station on the Potomac to Fredericksburg. In freezing rain and cold, several died of sickness, nine in a few days.

On December 9th, just after midnight, the First Corps, under General John Reynolds, whose three divisions included Doubleday's, composed of four brigades, one of which was the Iron Brigade, marched off towards Fredericksburg. They were delayed by the crush of Federal troops on the road, and it was not until 5:00 A.M. on the 11th that they started again for the Rappahannock, marching downstream nearly two miles to Franklin's Crossing. Two pontoon bridges had been set up there, but they had to wait until the morning of the 12th to cross, until Federal skirmishers had driven off the pickets on the other side. Across the river, the First Corps split, some going up river towards Fredericksburg, following the Sixth Corps. The Iron Brigade was among those turning downstream, and for once, found themselves on the extreme Federal left, nearly out of the battle. After a cold night, Burnside ordered an advance, but the Iron Brigade and the rest of Doubleday's Division came under a Confederate artillery barrage from Jackson's right in the woods above. They were shelled heavily, as Partridge reports, and could do little but take cover. Battery B set up and returned the fire. The Twenty-fourth Michigan, eager for battle, attacked and captured some of Stuart's cavalry, and attacked also a band of sharpshooters harassing another Federal battery.

Things went much worse on the Federal right, where Burnside tried again and again to storm Marye's Hill south of the city, with staggering casualties. Unable to advance, Burnside stayed put all of the 14th, and with small truces, managed to bury some of the dead and to rescue some of the wounded. At night on the 15th the Army of the Potomac withdrew across the river. Pickets were left out to mislead the enemy, and most, at least those on the left, managed to scurry to the boats left by the Engineers after the pontoon bridges were cut loose. The Nineteenth Indiana, deployed far down river, also raced to the boats and made it.

Partridge is glad to get back safe. The Brigade had 65 casualties, 32 of them from the Twenty-Fourth Michigan. They have earned their black hats. Battery B had eight casualties, losing two men, eight horses killed, and six men, five horses wounded. The Army of the Potomac lost 12,600 men, killed, wounded, and missing, of the 120,000 sent across, and gained nothing; the Confederates, from their defensive positions, lost 5,300.

On December 20th, the Army of the Potomac set up camp near Belle Plain, near the Potomac, twelve miles east of Fredericksburg. On the 23rd, the Iron Brigade arrived, and set up camp overlooking the Potomac. Partridge describes the shanty they have built, typical of the rest of the enlisted men's quarters.

WINTER IN CAMP, TIRED OF THE WAR

20.   Celia Slocum and Evaline Slocum   (Erie)

Camp near Belle Plaine
Jan 14 1863

Dear Sisters
    I receaved a letter from you a few days ago but could not an-
swer it until now as we had to go out on Picket
    Well I dont know as there is much news to write this time..
we did not see any thing out on Picket to scare us and had a very
good time.   We have been puting up winter quarters here   my-
self and three others have got a shanty 6 feet by 12.   have a small
fire place in one side   I think we could stay here all winter very
comfortably if they would let us   but know knowing how long
we can stay here
    Well it is getting late and the wind blows in the house so that I
cant see very well so I guess I will quit for tonight

Jan 15

    Good morning to you.   this is a fine morning but the wind
still keeps blowing.   now I will try and finish   I will not say
much about the war for I only wish I was a Commissiond Officer
so that I could <u>resine</u> and you may <u>Bet</u> I would get up some ex-
cuse to resine   for I dont want to fight for the <u>Gentleman Negro</u>
any longer..
    Well I cant find any of the Penn Regts or rather cant get where
they are   they are all under Seigle.   and are some 30 or 40 miles
from here..
    You want to know what kind of country it is around here..
well around here it is very hilly but around Fredericksburgh it is
more level   it is not much of a farming country around here..
    Well I cant think of much more to write this time.   I receaved
a letter from home a few days ago   all well up there   also one

from Cousin Louisa   all well there.   I have not heard from
Waukegan in some time.
　　　Well I guess I will quit as I have two more letters to write   so
good by.
　　　from your Brother   G. W. Partridge jr   C. M. Slocum

P. S.   tell Frank I will write to him another time.   I send him
my best wishes
　　　　　　　　G. W. P.

It is curious that two days after telling Cordelia Howe and Phebe
Holdridge about the Fredericksburg battle and the terrible shelling
there that Partridge does not tell Celia Slocum a word about it, not
even that he is unharmed. He does say that he doesn't want to talk
about the war. This is as discouraged as Partridge has been, and the
spirit seems to have gone out of him. Nolan cites several angry and
discouraged comments from Iron Brigade soldiers about the futility
of the Fredericksburg campaign.[35]

Partridge's remark about not wanting "to fight for the <u>Gentleman
Negro</u> any longer" seems out of character. He has never expressed
any opinion on slavery in his letters. His motivation for volunteering
has never been strongly expressed, either, but he has implied his
support for preserving the Union. A photograph in *The Iron Brigade*
shows a black cook among some non-commissioned officers in the
field, so it is probable that Partridge has had some exposure to ex-
slaves while in the army. The term "Gentleman Negro" is a mocking
of abolitionist sentiment, however, and probably a common response in camp to the zeal of those with abolitionist leanings. It is
also an attempt to find a scapegoat for the war and its hardships, to
shift blame from the beneficiaries of an evil institution to the victims
of it. Partridge was closer to the source of his hardship when he
characterized the opposing soldiers as devils, or when he struck out
at the incompetence of his military leaders.

---

[35] Nolan, p. 187.

21.   Cordelia Howe and Phebe Holdridge   (Waukegan)

Camp near Belle PlaineVa
Janr 18/63

Dear Sisters
    Your kind letter of the 16th ult has just got along   it found me still in good health and I hope these few lines will find you the same.
    Your letter was delayd on the road just as I thought or I should have heard from you before   I wrote a letter to you a few days ago to know the reason but now I can see.
    Well I went through the great battle without being hurt although our Regt did not get into the fight very hard but were shelled pretty bad some of the time
    Well a little about the weather   we have had very fine weather all the winter so far   very little rain   freese hard most every night..
    I believe I told you in my other letter about our winter quarters and now we have a <u>fair show</u> for leaving them.   we have orders to have two days rations cookd by night but I dont know as we will move yet.   <u>I hope not</u>..   Well as I suppose you know I wish this war was ended for I am tired of fighting for the <u>Colored Gentleman</u>.   if I was a commissiond officer I would resign if I could   but I am not nor dont expect to be as lond as I stay in the army..
    I am going to send Hatty a small Present   it is not very costly but as some of the boys were getting them to send off I thought I would do the same   it is a gold Pen   it is a small one   I sent to New York and got it   I dont send it to make her write more but as a present   Well I dont think of much more to write this time..
    Them Postage Stamps you sent got through all safe   very glad to get them but since we were paid I have sent most all of my money off so I am short now but expect to be paid again soon   I

will see if I can get any Change of any of the boys.   if not I will send it next time   So good by for the present

C. S. Howe and E. P. Holdridge

G. W. Partridge jr

The mail is not always reliable. The late letter Partridge receives presumably asks about the Battle of Fredericksburg, and how Partridge has fared in it. He repeats briefly what he has related in more detail in his letter of January 12th.

The orders to prepare two days' rations presages another disastrous expedition which Partridge will describe in his next letter.

He expresses his discouragement as he did to Celia Slocum four days before, but seems to brighten a little as he describes the present he is sending to Hattie. Apparently, she has written as he has asked.

22.   Cordelia Howe and Phebe Holdridge   (Waukegan)

Camp near Belle Plaine Va
Feb 4 1863

Dear Sisters
    *Yours of the 27th was Duly receaved and you may be sure I
was glad to hear from you   yours found me in good health and I
hope these few lines will find you the same   I cant think of much
news to write this time   We were out on picket yesterday and day
before   it was very Cold last night and it is Colder this morning.
the wind blowd so hard last night that it took a part of the top of
our house off..*
    *We have had some rough weather here since I wrote before..
on the 27th it commenced raining.   raind all day and all night.
the next morning commenced snowing.   snowd all day   melted
as fast as it come.   snowd all night and frose up in the morning
the snow was 6 inches deep.   the storm stopt   the snow did not
last long..*
    *I must give you a little sketch of our march   I cant give much
for it is to cold   we started on the 20th   had a fine time that day
it commenced raining that night and it raind hard all night..   at 9
oclock in the morning we started again.   raining hard all the
time*
    *We marchd until about 4 and found all the army that was
ahead of us <u>stuck in the mud</u>   raining some yet.   we stopt there
all night and all the next day and next night.   on the morning of
the 23rd we started on the <u>back track</u>   mud about knee deep
some of the way.   every hollar that we came to we would find 2
or 3 waggons stuck fast..   Well we got back to our old Camp that
day and found the 17th Conn in it   they moved out the next day
and we moved in and here we are <u>safe and sound</u> and I dont care
about trying it over again until the roads get better..*
    *Now a little in answer to yours.   you wanted to know our
Colonels name   his name is W. W. Robinson.   we are in*

Wadsworths Division   the same Division we have always been in but a diferent Commander..

As to the question you have asked   for my part I dont know what was the matter with her   I was not at home much of the time and never heard any one say any thing about it..   Now dont think that I know and wont tell you for I dont know

Well I Cant think of any more this time   you must excuse this Poor writing for if it was as cold where you are as it is here I dont think you would write much..   we dont have to carry our wood very far here   only about half a mile and up hill most of the way that is not much for a Soldier   but it would be for a Colord Gentleman.   I expect we will have to wait on them someday well that will do for this time

So good by for the present   write soon   and I remane as ever your only Brother

George W. Partridge jr

to his Sisters   C. S. Howe

&

E. P. Holdridge

Partridge describes the infamous Mud March, which, following the disastrous assault on Fredericksburg, cost General Burnside his job. On January 26th, Burnside was relieved and replaced by General Joseph Hooker, who had been commander of the First Corps at Antietam, and had been wounded there. He set about to try to restore morale in the Army. He instituted furloughs, brought pack mules to reduce the amount soldiers had to carry, passed out special insignia to Divisions (a red circle was issued to the First Division, First Corps, which members of the Iron Brigade placed on their hats), instituted a system of resolutions concerning aims and purposes, attitudes towards conscription, Northern dissenters, support of the Union, and other slogans, which the soldiers affirmed by acclamation at all levels, and, most importantly, he improved the food greatly in quantity, quality, and variety. The Iron Brigade also got a new Division Commander in General James Wadsworth, while General Abner Doubleday moved to command the Third Division.

When Partridge says, "I dont know what was the matter with her," he is probably referring to his sister, Mary Ellen Tanguey, who had died in March of 1861, but Partridge knows nothing further, nor do I.

Partridge's final remark, "I expect we will have to wait on them someday," sounds like more camp talk, and will be the last of this sort. General Hooker's new regime will restore focus.

23.   Celia Slocum   (Erie)

Camp near Belle Plaine Va
Feb 28th 1863

Dear Sister
   your letter of the 21ts maild was receaved this morning and I was very glad to hear from you once more.   yours found me still in good health and I hope these few lines will find you the same..
   there is not much news to write this time..   the most of the Regt is out on Picket   we have to go on Picket about once a week. the weather here is about the same as it is up there.   we have some sun and considerable snow and good deal of Rain and an Awful [lot] of mud and take it all in all it is not very pleasant much of the time.   we had about 8 inches of snow a few days ago and now it is all gone   myself and a few other boys went out a while ago and found a Bee Tree.   we cut it down and got quite a lot of honey out of it with very little work..   I suppose you get most of the __War news__ now better than I can give it to you..   you say one poor cuss of a "soger" Came home.   that makes me think how there was seaven went home from our Camp.   I dont know wether they went home or not.   I think __not.__   there was five men Court marshaled and sentenced to have their __heads shaved__ to forfeit their Pay that is due them and all their __Bounty__ and have the Buttons tore off from their Coats and Drumed out of the service to the tune of the __Rogues March__ all in the presence of this Brigade I can tell you it was an awful sight to look at or to think of
   I never want to see another such a sight and hope I never will have the Chance..   I did not tell you what all this was for.   it was for __Deserting__ and getting __Catchd__ again.   they are to be passd out side of our lines that is out side of Baltimore..
   I see you direct your letters in care of Captain Stevens.   he is not our Captain now nor has not been for almost a year.   I thought I had told you of it once but dont know   however I now

tell you.. the Captain we have had since that was Capt Drake but he has gone now   he resigned about two weeks ago..

*   you speak of Oliver Braging that I sent them some money. all the money I sent them was some to pay for some Postage stamps that I sent for.   that is nothing more than I will do to any one that will send them   if they make their Brags to much I wont send them any more[,] stamps or no stamps..   tomorrow we are to [be] mustered for four months pay again but I dont know how soon we will get it..*

*   you say you dont see any of Ev's letters   if so you must not let her see any of yours   and again you [say] you dont know as it is any of your business what they do.   well I dont know as it is but it dont do any hurt to speak about it some times..*

*   Well as I suppose you know I still wish this war was ended but dont know when it will be   I dont see any sign of it ending yet or at least not much..   I think if we get Vicksburg it will be a hard Blow on them   I expect every day to hear of it being taken but dont hear it yet*

[No close for this letter—perhaps it is incomplete.]

Partridge seems to be recovering his joy in life. His finding the Bee Tree is a small event, but obviously gave him pleasure, and it pleased him to report it.

The court-martial sentences of the deserters makes a solemn impression on Partridge, as it did on others in the Brigade. Another Seventh Regiment soldier wrote in his diary an even stronger reaction: "I should much rather face the enemy than to witness another such scene."[36]

Oliver is Oliver Slocum,[37] Celia Slocum's father-in-law and Evaline Slocum's husband. There is some friction between these two families of unknown cause, but Oliver is teasing Celia, who takes the bait, and Evaline is no longer sharing Partridge's letters with Celia.

---

[36] Currier MSS, diary entry Saturday, February 21, 1863.
[37] Oliver Woolley Slocum, 1800-1871. Born in Otsego County, New York.

None of these unshared letters has come down to us. Partridge tries gently to mediate.

Partridge is no longer wishing he had a way to get out of the army. He wishes only that the war were over. He is interested in hearing good news from Vicksburg, which "will be a hard Blow on them." On the Confederacy. He has found the enemy again.

24.   Cordelia Howe and Phebe Holdridge   (Waukegan)

Camp near Belle Plaine Va
Mar 2nd 1863

Dear sisters
*   Your letter of the 24th Ult has just arived and haveing nothing els to do at present I thought I would answer it.   there is not much news to write this time only that we are all well and I hope these lines will find you the same   you say that Howe has got home.   well I am glad of it if he doesnt have to Come back again and I hope he wont.   you speak of some men Deserting.   if they are found again they will have to suffer for it.   there was five men Tryed and Condemnd for Deserting from this Brigade.   they had to have their Heads Shaved and Forfeit all their pay and Bounty and be Drumd out of the Survice of the United States all in the presence of this Brigade.   there was not any out of this Regt.   I tell you it was a hard looking.   I never want to see any more such sights and hope I never shall have occasion to*
*   well a little about the weather   it has been pleasant some and stormy a good deal   we have had some snow some rain and a great deal of mud   the snow was about 8 inches deep one spell here but it did not last long.   today is a very warm pleasant day. I had a letter from home a few days ago   all well up there· and one [from] Celia   all well there*
*   Well I cant think of any more to write this time   Best respects to Howe & hattie and all the rest of the folks.   write soon*
*   from your Brother   Geo W Partridge jr*
*   C. S. Howe.   E. P. Holdridge*

Partridge is hearing of deserters from both Erie and Waukegan, and repeats his account of his moving experience in watching court-martialed deserters "Drumd out of the Survice of the United States all in the presence of this Brigade."

25.   Cordelia and William Howe   (Waukegan)

Camp near Belle Plaine Va
Mar 24th /63

Dear Sister and Brother
  your kind letter of the 17th was duely reaceavd and you may be sure I was glad to hear from you again.   yours found me still in good health and I hope these few lines will find you the same there is not much news to write this time   it dont look much like a move down here yet as it is raining very hard tonight.   I dont think we will move from here before the first or the middle of next month.   I am sure we wont if it keeps on raining as it has for the past week or two..   our Regt has to go on picket every 12 days and stay three days.   we have to go out again in a few days
  I suppose they are fixing to have a great Fight down at Vicksburgh.   we dont get much news from there now.   I think if we ever attact them here we will Clean them out.   I think Old Joe is just the man that can do it if his officers under him will do as he tells them.   we may not attact here but I think we will.   if we Cross we will go either below or above their Fortifycations..   what do the People think of the Conscription law up your way We all down here think it is a very good thing.   unless this war closes inside of four months   for by that time these 9 months mens time will be out and some of the two years men.   I think it was the most foolish thing Government ever done to enlist and Draft so many 9 month men   some of them their time is most out now and they have not done any thing yet   not enough to earn their bread.   there is one Brigade of 9 month men in our Division.   they have been in 6 months now and over.   and no prospects of their doing any thing yet.   they took the place of a Brigade of N. Y. men that were in for two years and their time is out in April.   the new Brigades time is out most as quick as the old one..   We have an inspection here three times a week.   Regimental inspection Sundays and Company inspection Tuesdays

and Fridays   you say you have been in seaven hard fought battles. well that is more than I have been in or want to go in. I have been in five and only three Victorious and one of them was Victorious only for a short time. that was at Gainsville

    Well I cant think of any more to write this time. tell Hettie I will write to her in a few days. give my respects to all your friends write as often as you can and I will do the same Direct as before

Wm. H. &. C. S. Howe

George W. Partridge jr

P. S.   it raind all night and orders have just come that we have to go on picket. a fine time we will have I think

G W P

Much of this is soldier-talk to his brother-in-law, William Howe. Partridge expresses confidence in General Hooker, but then, he also had confidence in General Pope.

Partridge affirms he has been in five battles, and calls Gainesville one of these, making the others Second Bull Run, South Mountain, Antietam, and Fredericksburg. South Mountain and Antietam he classifies as Victorious. If he was not in the Gainesville battle, which was not clear in letters 15 and 16, he is stretching things here to impress his brother-in-law. This is not characteristic of Partridge as we have got to know him through his previous letters. Also, his accounts of times, deeds, and actions in battle have corresponded closely to others' accounts, and have never sounded exaggerated nor glory-seeking. Besides, he is modest here—seven hard fought battles (Howe's terminology) is "more than I have been in or want to go in."

CHANCELLORSVILLE AND THE MARCH NORTH

26.   Celia Slocum   (Erie)

Camp of the 7th Regt
May 14 1863

*Dear Sister   your kind letter of the 8th Came to hand yesterday
and you may be sure I was glad to hear from you again.   but
sorry to hear of your having so much sickness in your family.
yours found me in good health and enjoying myself as well as I
ever did in my life.   well we have had another fight and Came
out all rite again.   our Brigade charged across the river hear (at
Fredericksburgh) and drove th enemys Pickets and Skirmishers
away from the bank of the river.*

*our Regt lost three commissiond officers and two or three Pri-
vates killed and wounded   other regts lost more   after we got
across the river we built some brest works to get behind in Case
they attact us there but we did not stay there   only three days.
we started for the right where the most fighting was.   we got up
there on Sunday morning just before the fight Commenced.   we
just [took] our position when the fight Commenced on the left of
us about a half a mile from us.   as good luck would have it we
did not get into the fight that time.   the battle raged about two
hours Awfuly   the hardest I ever heard it.   the enemy Charged
our brest works 7 times and every time they Charged our artilery
would Cut them down with Canister like grass.   while this was
being done our men charged on the hights at Fredericksburgh and
took them   the next day the enemy took them back again   then
the next day we recrossd the river and Came back down below
Fredericksburgh and here we are all safe again and ready for another fight and I think we will have it before a great while.*

*What do the People think of the Conscription Law up your
way   we think here that it is a good thing.   this war will never
be ended until we have more men down here.   the 9 months men
are going home from here every day.*

I dont know if I can get my likeness taken now as there is no plase to get it here.   if I Can get it I will do so but it is a poor show for any thing here

well I Cant think of any more to write this time.   I had a letter from home a few days ago   all well there.   write as often as you can and direct as before.   what is the matter with Evaline. Cand She write when your family is sick or what is the reason.   I guess she is getting lazyer than I be

good by for the present
from your Brother
Geo. W. Partridge jr
C. M. Slocum

Partridge has not written to Celia Slocum since February 28th. He relates another disastrous battle at Fredericksburg, although the major fighting takes place some 12 miles to the west, near Chancellorsville, after which this battle is named.

This was an elaborately planned attack with multiple crossings of the Rappahannock and Rapidan rivers. Lee had 60,000 men in and around Fredericksburg. Hooker commanded 130,000. The two major fords were Bank's Ford, four miles west of the city, and U.S. Ford, ten miles to the west. Hooker knew these were heavily defended, so he thought he would try a diversion. He planned to cross the Rappahannock by pontoon bridges at two places east of Fredericksburg, at Franklin's Crossing, a mile-and-a-half to the east, and at the Fitzhugh House Crossing, three miles to the east. He also planned to cross a major part of his army some 20 miles upstream to the west at Kelly's Ford. These troops would then march quickly south and ford the Rapidan, a tributary to the Rappahannock, at two places, to come in at Lee's rear. This would divert Lee's defenders at Bank's Ford and U.S. Ford so that a major Federal force could cross there.

The Iron Brigade was assigned to lead the way across below the city at the Fitzhugh House Crossing. They started at noon on April 28th from Belle Plain. With a stop to rest, they reached the river at 2:00 A.M. on the 29th as planned, to cross the two hundred yards of river while it was still dark. They were to drive out any Confederate forces on the southern bank, and to establish a beachhead so the rest of the Corps could cross. But the pontoon boats had not arrived, the same type of delay Pope had experienced in December. The boats arrived at 5:00 A.M., at dawn. As soon as the Engineers started putting the boats in the water, they were fired on from entrenched Confederates across the river, and had to withdraw. The Brigade returned the fire with rifles and artillery for an hour without dislodging the Confederates.

They were many hours behind plan, so Reynolds ordered a direct assault by boat. The Sixth Wisconsin and the Twenty-fourth Michigan were assigned to the boats, one company to a boat, with four men manning the oars. The remainder of the Corps laid down as heavy a covering fire as they could from the north bank. General Wadsworth himself, the First Division Commander, jumped in a boat while his horse swam across. The small Confederate force left their defenses and tried to scramble up the bank. A number were hit and a larger number captured. Nolan quotes a Sixth Wisconsin soldier writing long after the war: "The grandest fifteen minutes of our lives! *Worth one's life* to enjoy."[38] "Some may like to hear the music they make," Partridge had written about the bullets flying by him at South Mountain. Apparently some did. The Twenty-fourth Michigan lost 21 killed and wounded, and the Sixth Wisconsin, 16. 20 more from the Brigade were killed or wounded, presumably while launching the boats or defending the passage, for a total of 57 casualties during the assault. More than 90 Confederate prisoners were taken, and many guns.

The pontoon bridge was completed, and several divisions joined the Iron Brigade in building breastworks for the rest of the day and the next day, April 30th. Hooker's diversion had worked, and Bank's Ford and U.S. Ford were now uncovered for crossing. At 7:00 A.M. on May 2nd, the First Corps was ordered to recross the river and to march west to U.S. Ford.

---

[38]Nolan, p. 214.

Lee had split his greatly outnumbered army in two, and had sent Jackson far to the left to attack Hooker from the rear, similar to Lee's strategy prior to the Gainesville battle and Second Bull Run. Like Pope before Gainesville, Hooker thought Jackson was retreating, and ignored him. Hooker dug in, waiting for Lee to attack. Jackson attacked from the rear, inflicting heavy losses. Returning to his troops at night, Jackson was mistakenly shot and fatally wounded by one of his own men.

The First Corps had reached U.S. Ford by 10:00 P.M. and had set up camp for the night. They were roused at 2:00 A.M. and ordered across the river to replace the Eleventh Corps, which had been so devastated by Jackson. They arrived on the Federal right at dawn, just as Lee attacked on their left, as Partridge describes it, leaving the Iron Brigade unengaged, "as good luck would have it." The Sixth Corps and Gibbon's Division meanwhile had pushed through Fredericksburg, and by day's end, was close to Lee's rear. The following day, May 4th, Lee turned away from Hooker, counting on Hooker's remaining frozen in his defensive position, and drove on the smaller force of Sedgewick's Sixth Corps and Gibbon, forcing them to withdraw across the river at Bank's Ford on May 5th.

Hooker was not attacked on May 4th or 5th, and early in the morning on the 6th, Hooker ordered the Army of the Potomac to withdraw. The First Corps headed toward U.S. Ford. The Iron Brigade was the last to leave, starting for the north bank at 8:00 A.M. They marched in the rain and mud, stopping for the night opposite Fredericksburg, north of Falmouth, and reached the Fitzhugh House camp the next day, May 7th, where they had started from on April 28th. Nolan illustrates, through soldiers' accounts, the low state of morale in the Army of the Potomac.[39] Partridge, however, is happy he has come through safe, and that his regiment has lost only six men, and all of those at the forced crossing. On receiving Celia Slocum's letter on the 13th he states, "yours found me in good health and *enjoying myself as well as I ever did in my life.*"

---

[39] *Ibid.*, pp. 218-219.

At Chancellorsville, Federal losses were 17,000 men. Lee lost 12,600, more than he could afford. Chancellorsville has often been described as a masterful battle for Lee. Outnumbered more than two to one, he had met the enemy and had driven them off, giving more than he got. Lee had counted on the continued incompetence of Federal leadership at the top, and he was not disappointed. He had also counted on the continued success of attacking boldly. He would not always be so fortunate.

27.   Celia Slocum   (Erie)

Camp near Guilford Station
June 24th 1863

Affectionate Sister
I thought I would write a few lines to you to [let] you know how we are getting along.   the last letter I got from home was a few days ago   the folks are all well   I have not heard from Waukegan for a long time   I guess they have all forgot where I am or els they dont Care and if they dont I sure dont.
we have done some hard marching of late.   we left Fredericksburgh (our Regt) to go with some Cavelry to make a raid across the River.   we marched three days.   we had no fighting to do.   it was very warm and dry and dusty   in fact it was hot some of the time   after that was over we rested a Couple of days then the rest of the Brigade came up and we started again. marchd some of the time all night until we got to Centerville there we stopt one day and two nights and then Came up to this place.   we are now about 26 miles above Washington about 3 miles from the Potomac and about 8 miles from Leesburg   that is all I know about where we are.   I never was here before.
when I was at Centerville I saw one of my Cousins   one that I never expected to see   it was Cousin John A. Partridge.   I had wrote to him a few times   he is a very smart looking young man I wish he was in this Division.   he is in the 126 Regt N. Y. S. Volunteers   it was the first of my relation that I ever see since I enlisted.   I got a letter from Uncle William yesterday.   all well there.
I stood most of the march very well.   from Centerville up here I had a very lame back but Could not get a ride.   but have got about over it now.
well I cant think of any more news to write this time.   I wrote this with a pensil because my ink was all used up   I dont know as you can read it.

I will send George and Frank a specimen of our Change.   I
dont know but you get plenty of it up there   write as often as you
can   I suppose you dont get much time to write but write as often
as you Can and Direct as before
  from your Brother
    Geo. W. Partridge jr
    C. M. Slocum

Some of the early two-year enlistments expired in May and June of 1863, so that the strength of the First Corps was reduced from some 14,360 men to 9,400. Some shuffling of division alignment took place, and the Iron Brigade became the First Brigade of the First Division of the First Corps, a source of pride for them. General Meredith still commanded the Brigade, General Wadsworth, the Division, and Major General Reynolds, the Corps. The strength of the Iron Brigade was 1,883 men.

On June 3rd, Lee started north to take the war to Maryland and Pennsylvania. He could live off the lush farms there, and a victory in the North might enlist some help from abroad. With Stonewall Jackson gone, Lee reorganized his army into three corps under generals Longstreet, A. P. Hill, and Ewell, who had returned after losing a leg at Gainesville. Stuart continued to lead the cavalry.

Partridge describes a raid with his Seventh Wisconsin Regiment and some cavalry across the Rappahannock, starting out on June 7th. This was a sizeable expedition of 8,000 cavalry and 3,000 infantry under General Alfred Pleasonton, sent by Hooker to disperse and destroy J.E.B. Stuart's cavalry near Brandy Station, some 25 miles up river from Fredericksburg. Pleasonton and his small army marched up the Rappahannock and crossed at dawn on June 9th. Leaving the infantry in reserve,[40] the cavalry caught Stuart by surprise, and fought all day to a draw, recrossing the river at dark.[41] This was the

---

[40]Currier MSS, diary entry for June 9th, 1863. Currier states that "This morning we started and crost the Ford.... We was on the reserve all day," parallel to Partridge's account that "we had no fighting to do."

[41]Edwin B. Coddington, *The Gettysburg Campaign: a Study in Command* (New York: Charles Scribner's Sons, 1984). Coddington states, pp. 65-66, that

Battle of Brandy Station. On June 10th, the infantry proceeded to Bealeton Station, some four miles northeast of the river, and rested. The rest of the First Corps left the Fitzhugh House camp on June 12th, joined the Seventh Wisconsin at Bealeton Station on the afternoon of the 13th, and marching hard, reached Centreville on June 15th. They reached Guilford Station on the 19th, and stayed there until the 25th, when they started north again, trying to catch Lee.

Partridge had last heard from Cordelia Howe and Phebe Holdridge in late March, in a letter dated March 17th. He has evidently not heard from Evaline Slocum for some time. He feels hurt by this neglect, and lashes out, probably at Cordelia Howe, closest to him in age and affection. He tells of meeting John Partridge, his first cousin, who is twenty, in Centreville. He is his cousin Louisa Partridge's last of three brothers. John Partridge will die in a Washington hospital in the coming August. Uncle William is one of his father's six brothers.

Partridge has had remarkably good health while in the army. He has not been sick, and has never been wounded. His lame back is his first physical complaint, but he seems to have recovered.

George and Frank are two of Celia Slocum's sons, ages 14 and 11. There is no record that Partridge sent them any coins or other money. He asks his sister twice to write as often as she can, but it is unlikely that he received another letter.

This is Partridge's last letter.

---

two Iron Brigade regiments were among eight infantry regiments in reserve, which allowed Pleasonton to recross the Rappahannock uncontested. Neither Partridge nor Currier mentions a second Iron Brigade regiment. Partridge states, "we left Fredericksburgh (our regt)," implying that the Seventh alone of the Brigade left from Fredericksburg.

GETTYSBURG: THE FINAL BATTLE

ON June 25th, the First Corps, with the Iron Brigade the First Brigade of the First Division, left their camp near Guilford station at 8:00 A.M. and crossed the Potomac at Edwards Ferry at noon. They proceeded another 10 miles to Barnesville. On the 26th, they crossed the Monocacy River and Catoctin Mountain to Jefferson. On the 27th, they reached Middletown, near Turner's Gap, where the Seventh Wisconsin had lost 147 men at the Battle of South Mountain on the previous September 14th, and where Partridge had fired 70 rounds in the dark, aiming at the flashes from the Confederate rifles, and, ammunition spent, had lain down and gone to sleep. On June 28th, they backtracked to the southeast to Frederick, where they were surprised to learn that General Hooker had been replaced by General George Meade.

They marched on to Emmitsburg, and on June 30th proceeded north-by-east on the Emmitsburg Road into Pennsylvania, stopping at Marsh Creek at noon to make camp, some seven miles below Gettysburg. In late afternoon, a division of cavalry under General John Buford rode by to scout the roads ahead. At 8:00 the next morning, the First Corps continued towards Gettysburg on the Emmitsburg Road, Cutler's Brigade leading, followed by the Second Maine Battery, and then the Iron Brigade. Not long after they started they heard firing in the distance. General Reynolds rode ahead to see what was going on.

Ten roads converge on Gettysburg from all directions. Viewing Gettysburg from above as the center of a clock, the Emmitsburg Road came in from seven o'clock. The sounds of firing came from above the town, to the west, where the Chambersburg Pike came in at ten o'clock. Buford's Cavalry had met a strong vanguard of A. P. Hill's Corps, two divisions totalling 16,000 men on their way to Gettysburg, where they had heard there was a supply of shoes. Buford's men had engaged them out of town, bringing out a small artillery battery, and giving way as the Confederates cautiously advanced.

Reynolds rode towards the sound of the firing, out to Seminary Ridge, a long north-south ridge half-a-mile west of town which started a mile below the town. Shortly before the ridge crossed the

Chambersburg Pike was the Seminary itself, with a cupola affording a good view of the surrounding countryside. Reynolds climbed to the cupola, and was soon joined by Buford, who had ridden back to tell his findings. It was now 9:30. Looking from the Seminary up the Chambersburg Pike, Reynolds could see another ridge, McPherson's Ridge, some 500 yards to the west, also crossing the Pike. A hundred yards or so south of the Pike, McPherson's Ridge was covered with an open wood, no impediment to troops, but providing some cover. To the north of the Pike was a railroad cut through the ridges, with the track paralleling the Pike. This is where Reynolds decided he was going to fight. The Iron Brigade and Cutler's Brigade would absorb the first shock, but with the Eleventh Corps close behind, there would soon be 18,000 Federal troops, plus Buford's 3,000 cavalry, in strong position against A.P. Hill's 16,000, with another 16,000 Confederate troops in Ewell's Corps, reported by Buford's scouts, soon to be streaming in from the north. Reynolds knew the odds, and thought he could fall back from McPherson's Ridge to Seminary Ridge if pressed, and from there to a strong defensive position he could see below town, at Cemetery Ridge. He would hold back the Confederate advance at all costs until the rest of the Army of the Potomac arrived to secure the heights south of town. He sent a rider back to tell General Meade his plan, with other urgent messages to Federal forces scattered below Gettysburg, and rode back to hurry along his own First Corps.

At 10:00 A.M. the vanguard of the First Corps was a mile away, and left the Emmitsburg Road to follow Seminary Ridge north. General Reynolds met them there and proceeded to lead them toward McPherson's Ridge. He directed Cutler to move part of his brigade to the north of the Chambersburg Pike towards the railroad cut, where he was stopped by enemy fire. Holding the Sixth Wisconsin in reserve, Reynolds ordered the rest of the Iron Brigade to drive the Confederates out of McPherson's Woods. Four regiments charged up the slope to the woods and met heavy fire. In the fire, a Confederate sniper, probably from a tree, shot Reynolds dead. The Iron Brigade charged through and around the woods and drove the Confederates down the other side of the ridge, routing Confederate

General Archer's Brigade, capturing General Archer himself with 75 additional prisoners, and scattering the rest. Casualties were high on both sides. Cutler's Brigade faced the strong fire north of the Pike, but held on for a while, and then Wadsworth ordered them back to Seminary Ridge to regroup, along with the Second Maine Battery. Two of Cutler's regiments were kept just to the right of the Pike, but they soon fell back, leaving the Iron Brigade out in front alone. The Sixth Wisconsin with the Brigade's reserves, all led by Colonel Rufus Dawes, came quickly from the rear and turned the Cutler regiments back to the fight. Dawes led a charge across the Pike to the railroad cut where the Confederate brigade under General Davis was firing effectively from cover. After suffering extensive casualties in the charge, Dawes' men blocked the end of the cut through the ridge, and captured 225 men and 7 officers.

In some disarray, the leading edge of A. P. Hill's Corps fell back to reorganize, and the battle died down. General Abner Doubleday, at this time the only fit ranking leader for the First Corps, withdrew the Iron Brigade, Cutler's two regiments, and some of Buford's men, now fighting on foot, back to McPherson's Ridge and McPherson's Woods. Cutler's other three regiments returned from Seminary Ridge.

Ewell's Corps now arrived from the north and joined A. P. Hill's in front of the Federal First Corps, and at 3:00 P.M. the two Confederate corps launched an attack with artillery followed by infantry. The Iron Brigade held firm in the woods, but as Hill's troops swept round their left, they were gradually pushed back in a series of stands to a new line at the back of the woods. They fell back across the shallow ground between McPherson's Ridge and Seminary Ridge, and eventually to a new stand with the Fifth Maine Battery on Seminary Ridge. Late in the day, at 4:00 or 4:30, this position also gave way, and the Iron Brigade, again last on the field, withdrew in good order on the Chambersburg Pike to the center of town, turning south at the Emmitsburg Road to Cemetery Hill, where elements of the Eleventh Corps had established a strong position. The Sixth Wisconsin, along with the five regiments of Cutler's Brigade, which had been separated north of the Chambersburg Pike, also made their way back through town to rejoin the others. The First Division with the small remnant of the Iron Brigade was ordered to Culp's Hill, a half mile to the east, which, when secure, provided an impregnable base.

The First Corps and Buford's Cavalry Division had met the enemy first at Gettysburg, and led by the Iron Brigade, had held and delayed a far superior force long enough for Meade to gather together the full might of the Army of the Potomac, and to secure the strategic ground from Culp's Hill and Cemetery Hill, then south along Cemetery Ridge, to Little Round Top, Reynolds' brilliant plan,[42] taking the initiative forever from Robert E. Lee, and spelling the beginning of the end for the Confederacy.

Of the 1,883 men of the Iron Brigade who fought on July 1st, 1,212 were casualties, some 65%, most of them killed or wounded. The Iron Brigade led all Federal brigades in losses in the three-day Gettysburg battle, and in those losses, spent its identity. Somewhere between 10:30 A.M. and 5:00 P.M. on July 1st, 1863, and somewhere between McPherson's Ridge and Cemetery Hill, Partridge was shot in the chest and killed.[43] No records have been found of where he was buried. It has come down through family accounts that his body was identified through a sister's letter found in his pocket.

---

[42] Coddington, pp. 302-303. Coddington credits General O. O. Howard of the Eleventh Corps for the decision to secure Cemetery Hill. But Reynolds' whole point in holding the Confederates north and west of Gettysburg (at great sacrifice) was to allow time for the Army of the Potomac to secure the strategic ground south of town. His message to Meade, as reported (it was a verbal message), was specifically to this effect: "The enemy is advancing in strong force...I fear they will get to the heights beyond the town before I can. I will fight them inch by inch, and if driven into the town, I will barricade the streets and hold them back as long as possible." Freeman Cleaves, *Meade of Gettysburg,* (Norman: University of Oklahoma Press, 1960), p. 135. Howard arrived at noon or shortly thereafter, after Reynolds was killed, but he met Buford and Doubleday there, both of whom knew Reynolds' plan

[43] Busey, p. 280. The listing is under the Seventh Wisconsin as "Patridge, George W.," as his name frequently appears in records. Like his Connecticut father, he probably pronounced it that way.

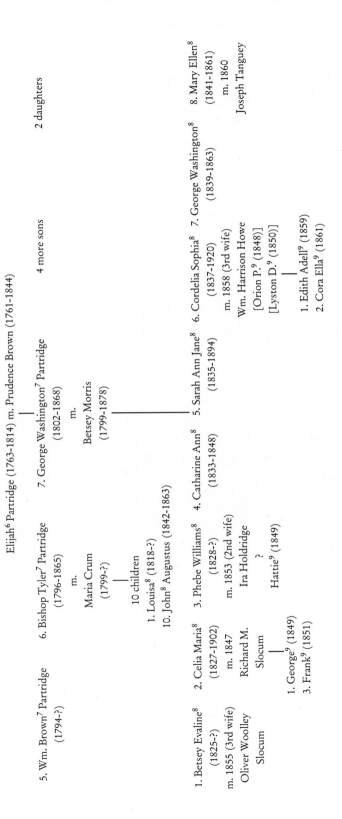

PARTRIDGE FAMILY TREE — 1863

Elijah[6] Partridge (1763-1814) m. Prudence Brown (1761-1844)

2 daughters

7. George Washington[7] Partridge
(1802-1868)

m.

Betsey Morris
(1799-1878)

4 more sons

6. Bishop Tyler[7] Partridge
(1796-1865)

m.

Maria Crum
(1799-?)

10 children

1. Louisa[8] (1818-?)

10. John[8] Augustus (1842-1863)

8. Mary Ellen[8]
(1841-1861)

m. 1860

Joseph Tanguey

7. George Washington[8]
(1839-1863)

6. Cordelia Sophia[8]
(1837-1920)

m. 1858 (3rd wife)

Wm. Harrison Howe

[Orion P.[9] (1848)]

[Lyston D.[9] (1850)]

1. Edith Adell[9] (1859)

2. Cora Ella[9] (1861)

5. Sarah Ann Jane[8]
(1835-1894)

4. Catharine Ann[8]
(1833-1848)

5. Wm. Brown[7] Partridge
(1794-?)

3. Phebe Williams[8]
(1828-?)

m. 1853 (2nd wife)

Ira Holdridge

?

Hattie[9] (1849)

2. Celia Maria[8]
(1827-1902)

m. 1847

Richard M.
Slocum

1. George[9] (1849)

3. Frank[9] (1851)

1. Betsey Evaline[8]
(1825-?)

m. 1855 (3rd wife)

Oliver Woolley
Slocum

Evaline Slocum, 59   Phebe Holdridge, 56

Celia Slocum, 57   Cordelia Howe, 47   Jane Green, 49

THE PARTRIDGE SISTERS, 1884

Celia Maria (Partridge) Slocum
Erie, Pennsylvania, about 1858, age 31, with son Edward

Cordelia Sophia (Partridge) Howe
Waukegan, Illinois, about 1875, age 38

By permission of Margaret Ferrell

Brigadier General John Gibbon

Lieutenant Colonel William W. Robinson

State Historical Society of Wisconsin

Pvt. Stanley J. Morrow
Seventh Wisconsin Volunteers

W. H. Over Museum

Camp of the Seventh Wisconsin Volunteers at Upton's Hill, Virginia, six miles west of Washington, D. C. The photograph was probably taken in early September, 1862, between the battles of Second Bull Run and South Mountain.

State Historical Society of Wisconsin

INDEX